A STEP-BY-STEP GUIDE TO INDEPENDENT PUBLISHING

Authority

Become an Expert, Build a Following, and Gain Financial Independence.

NATHAN BARRY

Authority: Become an Expert, Build a Following, and Gain Financial Independence
Copyright © 2014 Nathan Barry

All rights reserved. No part of this book may be reproduced or transmitted in any form or by any means, electronic or mechanical, including photocopying, recording, or by any information storage and retrieval system, without written permission from the author, except for the inclusion of brief quotations in a review.

Disclaimer: While the publisher and author have used their best efforts in preparing this book, they make no representations or warranties with respect to the accuracy or completeness of the contents of this book and specifically disclaim any implied warranties of merchantability or fitness for a particular purpose. No warranty may be created or extended by a sales representative or written sales materials. The advice and strategies contained herein may not be suitable for your situation. You should consult with a professional where appropriate. Neither the publisher nor author shall be liable for any loss or profit or any other commercial damages, including but not limited to: special, incidental, consequential, or other damages.

Editor: Lynn Weimar
Cover Design: Cari Campbell, Cari Campbell Design
Interior Layout: Fusion Creative Works

Print ISBN 978-1-61206-091-0
Library of Congress Control Number: 2013950431

First Printing
Published in the United States of America
Published by

Boise, Idaho
www.alohapublishing.com

Dedication

FOR MY SON, OLIVER

To show you there is a way to make a living that doesn't require a soul-sucking job.

Contents

Chapter 1: On Writing — 9

Chapter 2: Basic Marketing — 31

Chapter 3: Writing, Lots of Writing — 55

Chapter 4: Pricing & Packaging — 69

Chapter 5: Design & Formatting — 93

Chapter 6: Prepping for Launch — 117

Chapter 7: The Sales Page — 131

Chapter 8: E-Commerce — 139

Chapter 9: The Launch (and Beyond) — 159

Chapter 10: Closing Thoughts — 181

Start Before You Feel Ready — 185

Notes — 189

1

On Writing

Consistent writing is the single best thing I've done in the last year. It has transformed my finances, career, and business. Could writing do the same for you?

Why Write?

Have you ever played the game Marco Polo? It's a pretty simple game and it's the most fun if played in a pool. The rules are simple: one person closes their eyes and tries to catch or tag someone else. In order to find people, the person who is "it" can say "Marco" at any time. Everyone else has to respond "Polo." By listening to where the sound is coming from the person who is "it" can more easily find their prey. Once they touch someone else, the game starts over with the person who was caught now trying to find everyone else.

It's a great game. At least it kept ten-year-old me quite entertained.

What does this have to do with writing?

Well, nothing. Except that I want to talk about Marco Polo. The explorer, not the kids' game.

The Explorer

Marco Polo was a Venetian explorer who lived from 1254 to 1324 and became famous for being the first to explore the Silk Road to China. At least that's how he is remembered. There is only one small problem. He wasn't an explorer at all. Like all good Venetians of the time, he was a merchant.

Plenty of people had explored the roads to the East long before Marco Polo. In fact, Marco's father and uncle had made their exploratory trips well before Marco was born. So why does Marco get all the credit? Why is he the one we remember and name silly games after?

Simple. He wrote about it.

Those Who Teach

Think through the people who are well known in your industry. Why do you know who they are?

Are they the most talented? Sometimes, but often not.

Almost always it is because they teach. I know when it comes to web design (my industry), the people I had heard of were the ones whose books, tutorials, and blog posts I had read. They weren't necessarily the most talented, but they shared and taught everything they knew.

That's how they became well known.

You can continue to create cutting-edge work and strive to be the best in your industry, but until you start teaching and sharing, your reach and influence will be limited.

Teaching Web Design

In 2007, Chris Coyier launched a site called css-tricks.com. It was a site dedicated to teaching people how to code websites. (CSS is the language that describes how websites should look.) When CSS-Tricks first came out I remember reading a tutorial and arrogantly thinking, "I know that already." Chris and I were at about the same skill level, so I didn't learn anything new from him.

This continued for a while as he kept putting out new tutorials. But over time, as friends started asking me CSS questions, I found it easier to link to one of Chris's articles (since they were really well written) than explain everything myself.

Years later, Chris ran a Kickstarter campaign to redesign his site. Those who contributed would get behind-the-scenes access to additional tutorials and content related to the redesign.

The goal was set fairly low at $3,500. He quickly blew past the goal and by the end of the campaign had raised $89,697.

Incredible.

The point is that he did it with relative ease, all because he had built up an audience who loved his work.

He and I started at the same point and our skills progressed at about the same rate. The difference was he taught and shared whereas I kept what I was learning to myself. That made the difference between being able to make tens of thousands of dollars on a new project versus releasing to no one.

To Be Known, You Must Teach

Watching Chris's successful campaign, it finally sunk in that I needed to be teaching. My worth to the world wasn't in how well I knew CSS or how effectively I could code a website, but instead in how much value I could deliver to other people through teaching.

So I started to write my own tutorials and build my own audience. Within a year I had released two eBooks and made over six figures in profit from them.

The way I see it, you have two options: keep your skills and knowledge to yourself and be quickly forgotten (like the first explorers), or take the Marco Polo/Chris Coyier path and share what you've learned so that you will be remembered.

Which path is for you?

A Skill That Makes Money

It's not just about being remembered. Those who teach, under the right circumstances, can make a respectable income as well.

The main idea I want to leave you with from this book is this: if you know a skill that other people use to make money, you can make a living by teaching that skill. Most people think that teaching is for school. After high school or college the belief is that you are done learning, and now you can work.

But the truth is that to be successful you need to keep learning every day, whether you are a programmer learning new languages or a businessman getting an MBA.

In order to get promoted or take a business to the next level, new skills are required. When a developer learns a new programming language, he becomes more useful to his company, meaning he can make more money.

An Accidental Expert

An architect in Southern California wanted to find a way to make himself more valuable to his company. He wasn't being altruistic; he just wanted to be valued so that he would be promoted more quickly.

When looking at what made other architects stand out, Pat, the architect in our story, found the LEED certification for green buildings. Pat started to study for this very difficult exam, taking detailed notes as he went. Instead of putting these notes down on paper or a file on his computer, Pat put them in a program called WordPress. Using WordPress, Pat created a simple website to organize all his notes so that he could access them from any computer.

After months of studying Pat passed the exam and moved on with his life.

Then almost a year later the economic downturn hit the architecture firm Pat worked for and he was laid off. Since he had a few projects to finish up, Pat started to look at his options. During that time he started to learn about online marketing, which made him think about emails he had received recently about his study notes.

You know how Pat could access those notes from any computer? Well, they were put on a public website, so anyone could access the notes. That meant other people were using his notes to study also.

Curious about the emails he was receiving, Pat put a Google Analytics tracking code on his site, then waited until the next day. The results were incredible: four or five thousand people were coming to his site every day.

Search engines had indexed his notes and people were finding Pat's site through searches. Thousands of people were using those random notes—notes that most people would just put in a notebook and forget about—and using them to pass this exam.

Once Pat realized this and started to participate in his site, people asked questions.

Pat had become an expert without even trying.

Making Money

Since Pat was out of a job, he needed to find a way to make money. Ads were the first route he tried. First he tried Google text ads, but those didn't pay much money. Later he tried selling banner ads directly to companies with related products. That worked, but still didn't bring in a huge amount of money.

It wasn't until he took all his notes and packaged them up as a study guide that Pat started to make meaningful money from his site.

The guide wasn't new content, just the same content that was available for free on his site, but organized differently and distributed as a PDF. People were happy to pay.

In the first month, October of 2008, he made $7,905.88 in sales, considerably more than he had been making at his salaried job.

Sales continued to climb. Since launching the book Pat has made roughly half a million dollars in sales. And it all started with some study notes.

Pat learned a skill that other people used to make money and then made his own living by teaching the skill to other people. I did the same with software design. Better-designed software is easier to use and makes more money for the companies that own it, so developers who can create well-designed software are more valuable.

Just about every industry has new skills and certifications that are needed to advance in your career. Teaching those can be an incredible way to make money. You can also set much higher prices since it is easy for your customers to calculate a positive return on investment. We'll cover that in more detail later.

The difference between Pat Flynn and the thousands of other people who have taken the LEED exam is that Pat made his study notes available to the public.

Finding a Topic

Now you understand the value of writing, but how do you get started?

Well, you need something to write about. What do you know? Chances are, since you are reading this book, you already have something you could write about. But in case you don't, we'll cover that briefly.

What Do People Ask You for Help With?

A good place to start is by writing about an area in which other people perceive you to be an expert. What do your friends and family ask you for help with?

Is it setting up their web pages? Running a business? Fixing their appliance? Removing viruses from their computers?

If people are asking you for help in a particular area, chances are they think you know something about it. That also means there is demand for your knowledge. After all, not everything that could be taught has an audience of people who want to learn it.

You Don't Have to Be an Expert to Teach.

Even if you are learning a new skill or topic, you can still teach it. In all likelihood, someone will always know less about it than you do. Learning web design? Share your progress and write simple tutorials about what you've just learned.

After all, they say the best way to make sure you understand a concept is to teach it.

If you get in the habit of sharing everything you know, it will be much easier to position yourself as an expert later.

Just be transparent about your skill level and people will be happy to follow along and will even be far more likely to offer to help when you get stuck.

Establishing Expertise

I said earlier that you don't have to be an expert to teach, and that's true. Besides, who defines "expert" anyway? But if you want to make a living from your teaching, you should be perceived as an expert.

Creating this perception is far easier than you might think. Assuming you are actually good at your craft, a few quotes from past clients combined with some in-depth blog posts or tutorials is enough to give you the credibility to write your book.

Just the fact that you are writing a book gets you half way there. Seriously. Name your book, set up a landing page, and then start calling yourself the author of "X." People will take you a lot more seriously even before your book is published.

Working on The App Design Handbook is what transformed the perception of my blog from "an unknown designer writing about random topics" to "the author of a book on designing iOS apps."

There isn't some special club I had to join before starting to work on my book. You don't have to either. Just teach what you know, add as many credibility indicators as possible, and get to work. Ignore those who say you aren't qualified.

A Few Easy Steps

Tim Ferriss first showed me how easy it is to become perceived as an expert in his book *The 4-Hour Workweek*. I highly recommend reading the book for specific tactics and an overall mindset, but let me summarize his method (with my own variations) here:

1. **Join trade organizations with official-sounding names.** You need credibility indicators for people to take you seriously. A membership to a group is quick and easy. Designers can join the National Association of Photoshop Professionals. Listing that membership, even though it only costs $100/year, adds credibility.

2. **Read and summarize the top three best-selling books on your topic.** Completely original ideas don't exist. Everything you read is based on something else. So take

your favorite concepts from these books and write them from your own perspective. Turn these into blog posts. It only takes a few really solid blog posts for readers to perceive you as an expert. (More on that later.)

3. **Write for other sites and magazines.** Most news websites are funded by ads, meaning they need fresh reasons for visitors to keep coming back to look at their ads and read their content. For tech news sites this means up to a dozen new articles a day. Pitching a guest post or opinion piece is surprisingly easy—so long as you have something to say. Larger, more respected publications like Inc or Forbes will take more work, but that doesn't mean you shouldn't try. Wouldn't your resume look great to say that you had written for the leading publication in your industry?

4. **Give a talk at a local university and local offices of large companies.** I've spoken on design, web code, and marketing at Boise State University, not as a professor, but instead as a speaker at Boise Code Camp, a conference held at the university each year. I can still say I spoke at the university. You can extend this to give talks at well known companies as. The Microsoft office in Boise hosts a developer group each month. If you speak at that—which is not hard—then you've spoken at Microsoft.

5. **Piggyback on other people for press.** I've been mentioned or quoted in TechCrunch, Mashable, The Next Web, and plenty of other popular blogs, but none were directly talking about me. I've become good friends with the people who run Gumroad (my e-commerce provider)

and I promote their product any chance I get. Reporters aren't beating down my door to write about me, but they are writing about Gumroad every time they raise funding or hit major milestones. Each of those stories need quotes from Gumroad users, and the Gumroad team always refers them to me. I can now say I've been featured in all those places.

None of this is to trick or mislead people, just to demonstrate the necessary level of expertise so that people will take your book and content seriously.

Finding a Market

Two factors define whether or not your book can be successful. First, does it teach a skill that other people use to make money? And second, do those people gather and communicate online?

Now I don't mean that a product targeted at hobbyists can't be successful; it certainly can. I've purchased plenty of woodworking books—one of my hobbies—even though I will never make money from woodworking. But to get people to pay the prices needed to be really successful, it's best if they will use your training to make considerably more money than they spent.

It's also important that you can reach this audience. If they don't gather online in forums or on blogs you will have a hard time getting them to read your material. So if you can't find existing online communities in your niche, then this method probably isn't for you.

Keyword Research

An easy way to see if potential readers are searching for similar products online is with Google's keyword research tool. Just enter a phrase and see roughly how many searches it gets each month (https://adwords.google.com/o/KeywordTool).

Competition

When friends approach me with a business idea they usually excitedly say, "And there aren't any competitors!"

Yikes. That's not good.

What they see as a good thing, I see as possibly crippling their business. If there aren't competitors in your field you should ask why. When there are many successful competitors, it shows that there is a market. People are willing to pay for products and services in that niche.

I wasn't the first to write a book on app design. In fact, there is a great book called *Tapworthy* (published by O'Reilly) that covers app design well. The competition didn't affect my sales.

I was inspired to write my books by two other successful designers-turned-authors. Jarrod and Sacha's ebooks (I'll introduce you to them later) didn't make people less likely to purchase my book, *Designing Web Applications*.

Authority

Competition shows that there is a market. Embrace competition. See it as a good thing. There is plenty of room for everyone.

Be Consistent

Have an idea for a book? Congratulations! You've made it to the same place as 80% of the rest of the population. Turns out, just about everyone wants to write a book. But very few people actually do.

So what separates the wannabes from the published authors? Well, actually writing.

I wanted to write a book for years. In fact, I started several. And by "started," I mean I came up with a title, wrote an outline, and maybe a couple other pages. Then the project got put on the back burner, and I never came back to it.

Ugh! That's what a wannabe does. In order to become an author you need to actually write. Now you could write in random spurts of genius and try to finish your book that way, but that's unlikely.

Instead, I found that the best way is to make consistent progress every day. For me that meant making a commitment to write 1,000 words a day. Every day. I tracked this using an iPhone app I developed called Commit. Each day you meet your goal you track that day. Gradually, you build up a chain of days in a row. At first that is just three or five days, but over time it turns into a meaningful number. Then part of your motivation to stay consistent each day is that you don't want to break the chain. After all, skipping a day would mean that your days in a row count would be reset to zero.

As I write this I have 291 days in a row of writing 1,000 words a day. You can be sure that I am going to write 1,000 words tomorrow as well in order to not break my chain. The more you do it, the stronger the incentive to keep going.

Maybe maintaining a perfect streak of your habit isn't quite your thing, but the point is that to actually write your book you need to make consistent progress every day. It doesn't matter whether your daily goal is 100 words or 1,000 words; you just need to be consistent.

A decent length for an eBook is 25,000 words. If you were to maintain writing 1,000 words a day (which is really just 2 or 3 pages) for 30 days you would have 30,000 words. Do some editing and cut down your content (which is necessary), and you have a book written in 30 days. That's quite an accomplishment.

But what if you just can't put the words down on paper?

Writer's Block

Have you ever tried drawing and gotten stuck because you can't get a specific line right? The process goes something like this: draw, shake your head in frustration, erase, redraw, and repeat. I used to get stuck quite often writing and rewriting the same sentence. The problem is that if you erase your work and start over, you often repeat the same mistakes.

In drawing, you are far better off drawing your new line before you erase the old one. That way you can know how the new line needs to be different from the old, incorrect line.

The same is true for writing. Starting from scratch again and again won't get you anywhere. You need to write something and then edit it into its proper form. The editing can happen right then or you can put it off for later.

The one quote that made the biggest difference for me with my writing is this:

> "When faced with writer's block, lower your standards and keep going."
> - Sandra Tsing Loh

It's far better to write something than it is to write nothing while trying to achieve perfection.

Seth Godin claims he never gets writers block. Why? Because he writes like he talks. And, "No one ever gets talker's block."

You don't wait days to say something while trying to find the perfect way to phrase it. Instead you speak, hope the message gets across, and add extra explanation if needed.

We have much lower standards for talking, so we don't get stuck.

If you get stuck writing, lower your standards.

My Story

When I was growing up, I had the great privilege of being home schooled. For me that meant personalized attention, learning at my own pace, and ultimately being able to graduate a few years early. Once I learned that I had input in the speed and quality of my education, I became much more motivated. Rather than having to continue high school for a set number of years, I was given a fixed amount of schoolwork I needed to complete to graduate. I saw that as a checklist and dove in.

You shouldn't get the idea I was a perfect student. Far from it. I'm sure my mom could share a lot of stories, but I'll stick to just one.

When I was about twelve, I was working on an essay with my mom. Frustrated with the entire process, I exclaimed, "Why do I have to learn to write? I'll never be a writer!" My patient mother calmly explained something about how we need to be balanced in our skills and how writing is very important. I don't remember the details.

At a Christmas party a few months ago I met some of my wife's friends. Later one of these friends was talking to my wife and said, "I didn't know your husband was a writer." When Hilary, my wife, relayed that to me I was surprised. I'd never thought of myself as a writer. Sure, I'd written two books, but those were about teaching design. My focus was always on teaching.

That offhand comment reminded me of just how wrong I was while working on that school essay years ago. I did turn out to be a writer. In fact, even though I consider myself a designer rather than a writer, writing is the most important factor in my business.

I owe all of my marketing success, recent income, and lifestyle changes to writing.

I am also very thankful to have a mother who made me stick with writing and encouraged me along the way. Being a writer and copyeditor herself, she even edited my first two books (and this one, too!). So thanks, Mom. I owe you a ton.

Waiting to Be Picked

Have you ever felt that your success is entirely in the hands of someone else? The artist waiting to be discovered, the musician waiting to be signed to a record label, and the author waiting for a publishing deal come to mind as examples.

They are all waiting for someone to pick them, to say, "Your work is good enough."

But most people don't get picked. That's why the very idea of waiting can be so depressing. Everything is out of your control.

As an awkward kid whose friends were all older, I know what it's like to be the last person picked for a game. It sucks. That's why I don't wait to be picked.

I self-publish.

That means I don't have to wait for permission to start publishing my work and building an audience. Sure, I have to do more work. I don't have the support of a team, but I also don't have to wait for someone to pick me.

That's not to say I won't ever work with a publisher, just that I am not waiting for their approval to get started.

You can take control, set a plan, and execute on that plan to bring your own ideas to life.

Let me show you how.

Expert Interview

Start Small

Writing a book seems like such a daunting task. When I heard about book authors who spent years—even decades—writing their books, I figured it was nearly impossible to finish a book. And it often is, for certain types of books. But just because someone else spent thousands of hours on their life's work, doesn't mean you need to do that for your first book.

My friend Sacha Greif wrote, designed, and published his first book in three weeks. His book, *Step-by-Step UI Design,* is not a complete guide to designing software. Instead it is a guide that teaches you interface design through the process of designing a single application. Sacha's hands-on approach makes it easy to learn, and you see the results right away.

The entire book is only about 30 pages long, so it makes sense that it didn't take years to write. And that's just fine. Sacha sells it for $6, with a deluxe package that includes the source files for $12. That may not have been the best way to make the most money, but the book has done very well and opened up a ton of opportunities.

Best of all, had it failed (it didn't) he would have only been out a couple weeks' worth of effort (not years, like many first-time authors).

Sacha was kind enough to answer a few questions about his process.

Expert Interview

An interview with Sacha Greif, author of *Step-By-Step UI Design*

How long did it take you to write your book?

It took me about two weeks to write it, and then one week to format/edit it.

What inspired you to write a book in the first place?

Seeing the popularity of my post about designing the CodeYear.com landing page made me realize that there was a big demand for this kind of visual step-by-step design tutorial. So I decided to write a more in-depth tutorial, but this time try charging for it.

How much money have you made from your book and over how long?

I've made about $25,000 total over a period of one year, with a good half of that in the first month.

How has writing a book changed your business, career, or life?

It has changed my life in two ways. First, I became known as "that design eBook guy," which has both its good (people ask me a lot of questions) and bad points (they're always the same questions…).

Also, earning that much money in a short period of time enabled me to focus on personal projects like The Toolbox rather than take on new freelance clients.

Expert Interview

What marketing methods were most successful for selling books?

The only two things that had a serious impact on revenue were posting the book to Hacker News, and doing various deals with sites like AppSumo, Dealotto, and MightyDeals. Those were by far the most effective marketing channels, and combined they probably account for 90% of revenue.

How did you distribute your book?

At first I sold it on my site through Gumroad and Pulley, but then also did deals with AppSumo & Co. Although I'm aware of other distribution channels (like Amazon, for example), I haven't explored them yet.

What was the biggest surprise in the entire process?

Just how lucrative a book could be. I made more money with a single $2.99 eBook than most startups do over their whole lifetime. This is especially clear for me since at the same time I was also working on my own startup, Folyo, which never made anything close to the book's numbers.

The lesson for me is that the revenue potential of digital products in general (books, fonts, icons, etc.) is probably underestimated compared to the SaaS model that most startups favor. That doesn't mean one is better than the other, but it was an interesting realization nonetheless.

2

Basic Marketing

Marketing doesn't have to be full of meaningless buzzwords. The ideas we'll cover are targeted at promoting books, but also apply to just about anything you sell online. We'll specifically cover tools or training that help other people make more money.

Teaching

Once you create a product, how do you get people to buy it?

For the longest time I couldn't figure out the answer to this one question.

The obvious answer is through marketing, but what does that even mean? From the marketing books I read and classes I took in college, I learned that marketing meant brand awareness, focus groups, and audience engagement. What?

I saw how those ideas and buzzwords could (maybe) apply to 50-to-100-million-dollar companies, but I wasn't playing on those levels. I just wanted to find a way to reach a couple hundred people effectively. Marketing, as I knew it, was completely useless.

Marketing That Works

Without money for advertising, I had to find a way to get the attention of my potential customers. Fortunately there were plenty of examples to follow.

I watched 37signals, a software company that makes project-management applications, release a new product and immediately gain thousands of customers, all without spending anything on advertising. That's something I wanted to be able to replicate on a smaller scale.

So how do they do it?

Most people would look at 37signals and the first marketing thing they would notice is a blog with 100,000+ readers. Of course they can do it; they have people coming to them. If you think like that, you are missing the point.

37signals built that audience by teaching. They've written hundreds of blog posts about building businesses, designing software, writing HTML, and project management. By constantly teaching, they built an audience that came back for more and more content.

Then when 37signals launched a product, their readers were eager to give it a try.

Sound Familiar?

Does any of this sound familiar? That's because it's the exact same method Chris Coyier used for his Kickstarter campaign. Both Chris and the team at 37signals know well that if you start teaching, people will listen.

Then you never have to pay for advertising. Your audience comes to you. Give them enough value and they will happily pay you for more.

I used this method to sell over $150,000 in eBooks just in the last year. My only regret is that I didn't learn this simple lesson earlier:

Teach everything you know.

With our marketing principles in place, let's put together a way you can talk about your book, and potential readers can express interest in it.

A Landing Page

Does anyone want to read your book?

I'm glad you think so. But how do you know for sure? Before you spend months of your life creating something, you may want to test for some demand. My favorite way is to put up a landing page that enables your potential readers to tell you directly if they are interested in your book.

A Title?

Your first step is to choose a domain name. This can be frustrating since so many good names are taken. You should build one site to handle selling your book and showcasing all the content and blog posts needed for marketing. If you already have a blog, use that. There is no need to create an additional site for each product. In fact, I sell all my products and do my blogging on one domain: NathanBarry.com

By using a single domain I make sure that all links and content promote just that domain instead of splitting everything between several domains. My books live at nathanbarry.com/app-design-handbook and nathanbarry.com/webapps. This is much simpler and works great.

Using a single domain name means it can move with you as projects grow. This is why I like to use my name instead of something book specific. Personal branding can always be rolled over to new projects. Had I started with AppDesignHandbook.com it wouldn't have carried over well for my next product.

Many of my friends who started with book-specific names are transitioning to more personal branding so that their site works better for all their products.

Elements of a Landing Page

Once you have a place to host your site, you can use one of many WordPress plugins, Unbounce, LaunchRock, or my own company, ConvertKit, to set up the actual landing page.

Your landing page needs to have a few main elements:

- » A headline to catch visitors' attention (and keep them from hitting the back button)

- » An image and more detailed description of what your product will be

- » And most importantly, a way for visitors to express their interest. The best way is to have a field for them to enter their email address into, to hear when the book launches.

Let's cover these one by one.

The Headline

Is there a pain your readers have that you are trying to solve with your book? If so, your headline should speak directly to that. For Designing Web Applications I used the headline, "Are you scratching your head wondering why people sign up for your application, but never come back?" I chose this headline because I knew that was a painful point for software companies I talked to.

At this stage I wouldn't spend too much time on the headline. Just try for something that is clear and compelling.

The Description

Here, just get into more detail about your book. Who you are, why you are writing it, and when it will be available. If you have a sample chapter, outline, or anything else, feel free to include it, though I don't expect you to have too much information at this stage.

You know the feeling when you land on a page and think, "What the hell is this about?" Reading a headline can help you figure that out, but nothing is faster than seeing an image of a book to get you to realize that this page is about a book.

That's why I love including an image of a book—yes, a real-life, physical book—on my landing pages. Even though I am selling eBooks, the image helps the reader make an instant connection to my product.

The Opt-In

The last, and most important, part is to have an opt-in form. You can ask for name and email, or just email. It doesn't really matter, but don't ask for anything more. You are just trying to give your readers a way to show their interest.

If you want to get fancy (and increase your conversions) you can give them something for entering their email address. This can be something concrete like a free chapter of the book, a related article, or just a promise of a discount when the book comes out.

The goal is to have a little something that pushes them over the edge to expressing their interest.

Tell People

Now that you have a simple landing page (and I hope you didn't spend too much time on it, since it will change), it's time to tell people about it.

Taking Inventory

When my brother-in-law Daniel was thirteen or fourteen, I would often find him walking out of a random room in the house. Confused as to why he was in there, I would ask, "What were you doing?" He would casually shrug and reply, "Just taking inventory."

And he was. Later during a dinner conversation someone would mention that they were looking for something like batteries, and Daniel would jump in, saying, "Oh, you have some. They are on the top shelf of the closet."

It was a strange habit, but also very helpful at times.

Your Audience

You want to sell copies of your books, right? Well, to do that we need to take inventory of your audience, as well as your potential audience.

Start by making a list of all the methods you have to reach people who would be interested in your book. If you already have a blog, that is a great place to start. Beyond that, list any friendships with other bloggers in your target market, existing email lists, Facebook friends, Twitter followers, forums you are a part of, bloggers you are a fan of and could contact, and so forth.

This list is going to be the start of our plan to drive traffic to the landing page you just created.

Share the link to your landing page on any methods you control. Personally email all your friends you think would be interested, post on your social media profiles, and share it with any other online communities you are a part of.

Depending on the market for your book, don't forget about offline marketing as well. There are people who don't spend their lives online like you and I do (or maybe that's just me…). Talk to friends and club members, and just start looking for your audience.

Don't Be Afraid to Ask

Once you've exhausted what you can do on your own, it's time to ask your influential friends. I like to start by giving them a sample of the content that is highly relevant to their interests. At the end of that email, I ask them to share it if they found it interesting. Then I add an easy out, something that lets them know I am not expecting them to share it and that I just appreciate that they took the time to read the sample.

After *The App Design Handbook* (my first book) came out, I received a comment on my blog from an author who had written an ebook but hadn't sold many copies. He saw the success I had from asking my friends to share the link, but was hesitant to try it himself.

When I clicked through to his book I was surprised to see endorsements from some very well known individuals. Eighty percent of the people who had written a nice quote for his book I already knew and followed on Twitter. Basically, this gentleman had some high-caliber friends.

I encouraged him to ask his friends to share it, but with a soft sell. Ask for the favor, but give an easy way out.

He did. One friend shared the book on Twitter and it crashed the book's server—in a good way.

So don't be afraid to ask.

Setting Up a Site

This isn't a book about web design, but you will need a website, so I want to point you in the right direction.

Hosting

Since you should already have a name chosen from setting up a simple landing page, let's jump right into hosting. Both Bluehost and Hostgator are inexpensive options for low-traffic websites. Expect to pay around $10-$20 per month. If you want to get a bit more serious, I use Media Temple. Their prices start at $20 per month and increase significantly from there.

Don't fret too much over who to host with. There are many capable providers. Just keep in mind that comparing stats on storage space and available bandwidth is a waste of time. None of the low-end providers will actually let you use as much bandwidth as they advertise.

Install WordPress

You could spend months researching, testing, and installing different software to run your website. Don't. Just use WordPress.

WordPress is an open-source blogging and content management system available for free. In fact, WordPress powers over 15% of all the websites on the web. That's pretty impressive. Not only do you get a site setup for free, but you have access to a huge number of themes, plugins, and many experts who know WordPress inside and out.

All of the hosting providers I mentioned above have a one-click installation for WordPress. That's an easy way to get started.

Choose a Theme

Next, you need a theme for your site. You could have one custom designed, but that will cost between $1,000 and $5,000, which is probably not a great use of your money right now. Save that for when you have a best-selling book.

Instead you can choose from one of many free themes on WordPress.org or purchase a theme for between $30 and $100 from a premium theme company. Here are a few of my favorites:

- » WooThemes.com
- » StudioPress.com
- » PremiumPixels.com

When you buy a theme from any of these providers you can also get support from their forums, which could come in handy if you want to make any customizations.

Add Content

Now comes the most important part of your site: the content. Delete the filler content, write out a few pages, and start some blog posts. If you have questions, just try a simple Google search. The WordPress community is very large and always eager to help.

Just like that you have your own site—that you can edit—set up for less than $100.

Three Epic Blog Posts

Putting up a landing page is a really important step to capture interest and show people you are working on a project. But usually a landing page is quick, and because it has limited content, it doesn't do a good job of demonstrating your expertise on the subject.

That's where blog posts come in—three epic blog posts, to be specific.

Most Valuable

What's the most valuable thing you have to teach? That's what the blog posts should include. Don't be worried about giving away too much information or too many secrets. These posts are designed to get people interested in you and your book early on, so don't hold back.

Each post should be between 1,000 and 5,000 words long. Yes, that's a big range, but the length really depends on the content.

Become an Expert

You'd be surprised how little it takes to become perceived as an expert. A few detailed articles or tutorials will get you most of the way there.

Show Your Style

An author's teaching style is very important to know before you take a class from them. They may be an expert, but if they can't teach, they can't help you.

These first posts are a great opportunity to show off your teaching style. If that's your strong point you will really shine. If your teaching style needs work this is a great opportunity to practice.

If you have an established blog already, you may find existing posts that will meet these needs. Look for the posts relating to your book topic that get the most visits, shares, and positive comments.

If you don't already have a blog, this is a great way to get those first few posts going. Don't think you need a blog that has been around for a long time. That's helpful but not necessary. Starting off with some really strong, original content will attract the kind of readers who will be interested in a book on the subject.

That means these should not be list posts or aggregated content from other sites. Really teach. You are writing a book, so you need to be capable of original, long-form content.

Capture Leads

Here's the important part. At the end of each post you need to tell people about your book and give them a way to express their interest. Just like on your landing page, you'll do this with an email opt-in form. Here is an example from my book, *The App Design Handbook*.

This can go at the bottom of every relevant post on your site, but it is especially important on these epic cornerstone posts.

For increased conversion rates (the number of people who visit the site divided by the number who opt in to your form) keep the page really simple. The more options you give the user, the less likely they will be to take the one you want them to.

Why Email?

Both on the landing page and at the end of each blog post I advocate email opt-in forms. So you may be wondering why I think email marketing is so great.

Social media is all the rage. Everyone from small bloggers to international brands are using social media to improve their marketing. Twitter, Facebook, MySpace—well, maybe not MySpace—are helping marketers better connect with their audience. So as a new author that's where you should focus, right?

Social Media is a Waste of Time...

I thought I just needed to work hard to grow my Twitter followers, and then whenever I had something to promote thousands of people would flock to it. Turns out, only a fraction of your followers will even see a particular tweet or post. An even smaller number will actually click the link.

When I was promoting my iPhone app Commit I was thrilled to see it picked up by a popular blogger with about 80,000 subscribers each to her Twitter account and her Facebook page. That's a huge number! I was thrilled to see her posts mentioning my app go out to such a large audience.

Since Apple's App Store has a one-day delay on showing stats, I eagerly waited until the next day to see the massive spike in sales her tweet and Facebook post had generated. When I loaded the stats I looked and … nothing.

Not entirely nothing. There was a small spike, but that tweet had sold less than 20 copies of my $0.99 app. Later mentions on popular blogs would generate nearly $500 in revenue in a single day.

Getting someone with a popular Twitter account to notice your product is clearly not the path to riches.

… For Selling

Now I should qualify that last section by saying that social media is useless for selling. But it can be quite useful for building relationships with other people in your industry. I've met a lot of great people on Twitter and really enjoy having conversations and sharing content.

Just don't expect Twitter or Facebook to be an effective sales strategy.

Email Is Where It's At

One of my naive ideas when I started marketing was that the new tools (Twitter, Facebook, etc.) would work really well (they didn't) and that antiquated methods like email wouldn't work at all. Turns out, I had that entirely backwards.

Email marketing has been, by far, the most successful method I have used to sell books and promote products.

My love for email comes down to four main reasons:

1. **You can push content to your readers.** Instead of waiting for readers to check back for new content, you can send them an email each time you publish a new article. This is one benefit that is shared between email, RSS, and social media. It's important, but as you will see from my next few reasons, email is the best way for repeat connections.

2. **It is easier to get a visitor to enter their email address than to subscribe to an RSS feed or follow you on a social platform.** Since you can give out an incentive (a free ebook or a video tutorial) for subscribing, I've found it is far easier to get email signups than to get readers to follow you on other platforms. A short eBook I wrote and gave away for free, called the *Productivity Manifesto*, added 500 subscribers to my email list in just a few days.

3. **Engagement quality is higher.** Your email will be sitting in your reader's inbox next to important content from their friends, clients, family, and coworkers. Unlike social media, where most of the content is there to help you waste time, email is about getting work done.

4. **You have ownership.** Do you know anyone who built up a huge following on Friendster or MySpace? What's that worth to them now?

When you use another platform, you are at their mercy. If they change their rules, block your content, or die out, you lose completely. But with email you own the list. You can always move to another email provider if you don't like the one you are with.

I was talking with a friend about business assets a few months ago, so I started thinking through mine. I have simple stuff like a laptop, monitor, and some recording equipment, but that is only worth a few thousand dollars.

My website gets decent traffic, so that is worth quite a bit in potential revenue, but the core of my business is being able to contact my readers and customers, those people who have learned from my blog posts and purchased my books. They represent over a hundred thousand dollars in potential future revenue (if I continue providing value to them). All that potential lies in an email list of 6,500 people (at the time of this writing).

There is no way I am trusting my most valuable business asset to Twitter or Facebook.

Email Marketing Done Right

For many people, email marketing is synonymous with spam. Buying lists, scraping email addresses, and sending to people you don't have a relationship with are all spam. But that's not what we are talking about.

The goal of email marketing, when done right, is to provide immense value to your reader with each email.

In fact, you should make each email provide more value to your reader than for yourself.

What Email Lets You Do

My good friend Brennan Dunn is a master at effective email marketing. He started with a project management application for freelancers called Planscope. Through the process of growing and marketing Planscope, Brennan learned that freelancers also cared about increasing their rates and improving their businesses. Since he knew a lot about that topic, he wrote a book titled *Double Your Freelancing Rate*. (It's a great book.)

Brennan didn't have a popular blog or an established audience, but he did have email addresses for a few hundred freelancers who had tried Planscope. That means he didn't have to start from scratch. He wrote an educational email, meaning it provided value by itself and wasn't just a sales message, that also promoted his book. That's a great way to kickstart sales.

Then Brennan set up an email list with weekly tips and articles for freelancers. He invited the customers from both Planscope and *Double Your Freelancing Rate* to join the list. Over time, since he was giving out quality information, more and more people subscribed. Each week the content he wrote would promote one of his products while being useful by itself. I'm repeating this because it is so crucial.

A few readers on the Freelancers Weekly list started asking how to transition their freelance businesses into successful agencies, something that is very hard to do without losing money. Since Brennan used to run a million-dollar-per-year consulting business, he decided to help teach his readers how to do it successfully.

Instead of writing another book (that's a lot of work for just the few people that might need it), Brennan taught a two-day online masterclass on the subject. Tickets started at $1000 with 25 seats available.

Just like with his first book launch, Brennan didn't start promoting the workshop from scratch. In fact, he now had a list of over a thousand freelancers learning from his newsletter each week. Many were eager for this project. When he sent out an email announcing the new workshop, fifteen seats sold right away. Yes, you read that right. One email—with the proper lead up—generated $15,000 in sales.

Not yet convinced you should be using email?

All right, Brennan's story got better. He went on to sell out that workshop, and the one he did the next month. Brennan continues to do the workshop each month (just targeted at people on his Freelancer Weekly list). While it doesn't sell out every time, he has made over $90,000 in the last six months of running the workshop.

The takeaway from Brennan's story is that if you focus on email you never have to start from scratch with a new product. It works great for building an audience for the first product, and even better for connecting with your audience over the long term.

Brennan's latest book, called *The Blueprint*, helps freelancers and consultants find clients. He has since made over $20,000 on *The Blueprint*, almost exclusively from his email list.

If his story doesn't convince you to focus your online efforts on email marketing, I don't know what will.

Don't Let Your List Die

The most common way for email marketing to fail is when an email list becomes stagnant and eventually dies. This happens when the author builds a following or launches a product, but fails to keep things going afterwards.

If you do this, your readers will forget who you are, then be surprised to hear from you months later. This reaction is most often followed by unsubscribing.

Luckily, this problem is easy to avoid. Simply keep providing valuable content every week or every few weeks and you won't be forgotten. Even a good list will lose its value over time if neglected.

Expert Interview

Test for Interest

Jarrod wasn't sure if people would buy a book on design that he wanted to write, so first he designed a landing page that captured email addresses and pushed it live. After being featured on Hacker News the page brought in several thousand email subscribers—all before Jarrod had written any of the book.

An interview with Jarrod Drysdale, author of *Bootstrapping Design*

How long did it take you to write your book?

I took 4 months between announcing the ebook on a landing page and offering it for sale. I estimate about 2-3 months of that in writing time. The book is about 130 pages long. I didn't log my hours, though.

What inspired you to write a book in the first place?

I was inspired to write after learning about all the programmers who wanted to learn design, but didn't know how to get started. Obviously, the 30x500 process (Note: 30x500 is a product development class taught by Amy Hoy). But also, it seemed like my experience as a designer could be a big help to these people.

How much money have you made from your book and over how long?

I've made $56,416 gross, before Stripe processing fees and other expenses like MailChimp and web hosting. That's over almost exactly one year. (In twelve days, it will be a year.)

Expert Interview

How has writing a book changed your business, career, or life?

Writing a book has completely changed my business and career. My long term goal was to be running my own business, and now I'm doing that. I also have an audience I can launch new products to, which is incredible. It means I can continue running my own businesses long term. So I've been able to take my career in the direction I wanted to. I'm not sure how this would affect my employability. I don't really care—it's not really related to my goals. I've gotten some job offers because of the book.

What marketing methods were most successful for selling books?

For marketing, I started writing blog posts for HN and tweets to send people to a landing page with an email newsletter signup. Once I offered the book for sale, I continued doing that, but the newsletter became much, much more important. It drives a lot of sales.

Also, I write tons of personal email. Long emails to customers and people who are considering buying the book. I give design and business advice. I answer questions and share coupons. It doesn't have the highest return for time spent, but I think it does a lot to build loyalty and appreciation.

How did you distribute your book?

I sell the book on my own site using http://DigitalDeliveryApp.com and Stripe.com. I haven't even considered other distribution. I'm not really interested in it.

Expert Interview

What was the biggest surprise in the entire process?

The first big surprise was when the landing page lit up with traffic and I received hundreds of subscribers. The second and biggest surprise was when I earned $8000-$9000 within 48 hours of offering it for sale. There were lots of other surprises too: a customer calling me a "design guru" (I'm not), realizing how much writing I have to do just for marketing, and negative reactions from other designers.

If there are any other lessons learned, I'd love to hear them.

Another big lesson I learned was the value of humility and transparency. I know that a lot of people in our industry talk about this, especially the 37signals guys. But seeing it in action has been amazing. When people realize I'm just one guy working from his home office, their tone changes. People have been kind, appreciative, and helpful. They go way, way out of their way to talk about a little design ebook that's only sold a thousand copies. I've never experienced anything like it.

3

Writing, Lots of Writing

A book is a lot of work, but I want to show you how to make it more manageable. Slow consistent progress—along with a few other tricks—will help you meet your goal quickly.

What to Write

I don't want to start off by overwhelming you, so that's why I've waited until now to tell you just how much writing you have to do. It's a lot.

But it is totally manageable if you write consistently each day.

Here's an example of what you may have to write.

- » The book itself: 25,000-30,000 words (plenty will be cut from the final version)

- » Seven to ten guest posts at an average of 1,000 words each: 7,000-10,000 words

- » Three launch and update emails at 500 words each: 1,500 words
- » At least three posts for your own site: 3,000+ words

Of course your numbers will vary, but this should help set your expectations. Adding up the low end of our ranges we end up with 37,500 words. That's for a short book with minimal promotion work. Chances are you will be quite a bit higher than that.

In general, the more you teach, the more people will hear about your work, which will mean additional sales. Think of more writing as a good thing, not something to be feared.

Writing Order

Sitting down and writing a non-fiction book from start to finish is nearly impossible. Whenever I start a new book I don't know exactly what content I will cover or even the best order to cover it in. Figuring that out in advance would require far too much research and planning.

Instead, I create a rough outline, just bold headings for chapter ideas followed by bulleted lists for each of the sections. Spend an hour thinking this through and adding every topic you may want to cover.

Then create sections in your writing program (I do this in Scrivener) for each point on your outline, using folders to keep them organized by chapter. Don't worry about getting it right; you will change all of this later.

Now each time I start a writing session I just skim down my list until I find an interesting topic. Then I open that file and start writing.

This method lets me focus on writing in the areas I feel inspired, rather than not being able to move forward if I am stuck on a particular section.

There is plenty of time to edit later and get the order and exact content perfect.

Stand

I have a good friend who slouches further and further down in his chair as he works. Given enough time without a break he will disappear below his monitor, his head nearly level with his desk. He looks completely silly, the very pinnacle of terrible posture. Since he is a computer programmer, he spends a lot of time in that chair.

While I'm never quite that bad, poor posture has started to become a problem for me. Not good.

A great solution for me has been to stand as I write. In fact, I'm standing right now.

No, I didn't invest in a motorized desk that raises and lowers. Instead I just used a bookshelf in my office. My laptop goes on the top shelf, my keyboard on a lower shelf (propped up on a hatbox, if you must know). It's not going to get featured in any beautiful office space blog posts, but my ghetto setup works.

In addition to fixing my posture for short writing segments, it also has worked wonders for my focus.

You know how all the trendy software companies have implemented "standup" meetings?

When you are sitting it is easy to get distracted and seem like you have plenty of time. Checking Twitter, approving blog comments, and reading a few articles can quickly spiral out of control to ruin a work session.

Standing is different. You want to get the task done and move on. Standup meetings are designed to be short and efficient. Standup writing is the same way.

I also don't have a mouse in this setup. I can use my laptop track pad to do some quick navigation, but since it is near shoulder height it is uncomfortable for extended use, forcing my hands back to the keyboard where they belong.

Not all my work is done standing, but I find it is the best position for writing.

Research Can Be Fun

Sitting by the pool at a villa in the hills outside of Florence last summer, I was thoroughly enjoying myself. It wasn't just the sun and a view of the Italian countryside that made the evening so nice. I was also doing research.

It would have been better if just lounging by the pool could be considered research, but I had to be reading as well. I was reading a book on designing iPhone applications, carefully taking notes on my iPad, all to make sure I didn't miss any topics for my own new book on the same subject.

Before writing any new book I read as much as I can from other authors on the topic. The goal isn't to copy their work, but instead to make sure I'm not missing anything important. I find examples in their books to inspire my own stories and examples from my own work history to illustrate a point.

As you write your book, keep learning. In fact, never stop learning. There will always be someone who knows more on the topic than you do. Learn from them. Cite them in your book, read the source materials they learned from, and use their work to inspire you to make yours even better.

Planning the Final Content

For each of my books I have a target length of about 25,000 words. This is specific to the style of books I want to write. Don't add fluff just to meet a word-count goal, but know the approximate page length where you think you will have said everything necessary on the topic.

Since my writing tends to be scattered sporadically throughout the book, I wait until I near this goal before stepping back and reviewing everything I've written. For *The App Design Handbook* I reached 18,000 of my projected 25,000 words before taking a step back.

Inevitably, my manuscript has overlapping content, stories that aren't relevant, and ideas that are still entirely missing. The point of this step is to identify those and work to fill in the gaps.

Book Wireframes

In software design there are many ways to solve the same problem. Many will work, but they are not all equally good. It is important to try out several interface ideas to see which solves the problem best. To do this quickly I recommend that you create wireframes—simple sketches that convey the high-level ideas—to try out many ideas quickly.

Organizing a book works in the same way. The arc of your book could be arranged in several different ways while still conveying the same message. You need to plan out your sections and chapters. Then try out different organization methods.

There are two obvious ways this book could be organized. Option one is by topic. First we discuss planning, then writing, then marketing, and finally sales. That makes all the information on each topic easy to find, since it is grouped together. But that doesn't take into account the order books are written in.

Option two is to follow the book writing process, first with planning the idea, then initial marketing, then more on writing the book, followed by stepping up marketing efforts, and finally into packaging and launching the book.

To solve this dilemma I would open a blank document and organize the book in every different way I could think of (without wasting too much time), then choose between them.

Make sure to look beyond your first impression in order to find the best way your book can be organized.

Cutting Content

The last thing you want to do is waste your reader's time. Cut unnecessary sections, remove duplicate ideas, and get straight to the point.

Keep in mind that the content you cut does not need to be wasted. You will need tutorials, stories, and lessons for use in guest posts and teaser articles. When you are forced to cut content you really like because it doesn't fit perfectly with the rest of the book, try to find a place outside the book to publish it.

Filling in the Gaps

Eventually you will reach a point in your writing process where you can't think of anything more to say. But did you cover the topic thoroughly?

Start by reading through your content to see if gaps come to mind. Then go back and look through all your blog posts and other writing on the subject. Is there anything you forgot to include?

Next, turn to your readers. I hosted an hour-long online question and answer time with my Twitter followers in order to get their questions. I then had a list of things I knew people considering self-publishing wanted to know. Then I made sure each relevant question was answered in the book.

Finally, I turn to my research, skimming back through the books and articles that inspired me in the first place and writing about any forgotten topics.

Naming the Book

Naming products is hard. As creators we tend to overvalue a great name and spend too much time trying to come up with one. For my first book I tried to find an original, witty name for weeks before eventually settling on *The App Design Handbook*. It's clear and straight to the point.

Brandon Savage wrote a book on object-oriented PHP titled, *Do This Not That: Object-Oriented PHP*. While the book sold well at launch, sales quickly tapered off. After receiving feedback that the name was too "clever" and didn't communicate what the book was about, he tried to find a clearer name.

He eventually settled on *Mastering Object-Oriented PHP*. That name isn't going to win any awards for an original title, but it clarified what the reader will get out of the book. Brandon immediately noticed an increase in sales after changing the name.

> **"Be clear first and clever second. If you have to throw one of those out, throw out clever."**
> - Jason Fried

Jason's point applies just as well to book titles. I always wanted a clever title for my books, but decided to be even more straightforward for my second book about designing web applications. Any guesses what the title is? Yep, that's right: *Designing Web Applications*, which hasn't hurt sales at all.

Be clear first, clever second.

Focus on Outcomes

How will your readers' lives and work be different after they implement the ideas in your book? Will their career change? Will they make better products? Can they quit their job?

Outcomes like these are a great place to start when thinking of book titles. List out the benefits under the categories of career and lifestyle. Often you can find a title in those ideas, or at the very least a subtitle.

Brennan Dunn could have called his book something about how to market your freelancing services and win more client projects, but instead he used a very clear outcome as the title: *Double Your Freelancing Rate*. I'm not sure it is possible to be any more clear as to what your book does.

Formulas

I really don't want you to waste time on a name, so here are a bunch of formulas with examples you can use to quickly name your own book:

- » _____ Handbook (The Risk Handbook)
- » Bootstrapping _____ (Bootstrapping Design)
- » Mastering _____ (Mastering Object-Oriented PHP)
- » Hacking _____ (Hacking Design)
- » Step-by-Step _____ (Step-by-Step UI Design)
- » _____ Bible (The Web Copywriting Bible)
- » Learn _____ from Scratch (Learn Web Development from Scratch)
- » _____ Survival Guide (The Designer's Survival Guide)
- » Introduction to _____
- » How to _____
- » Professional _____ (Professional Web Design)
- » _____ for _____ (Color Theory for Startups)
- » Principles of _____
- » The _____ Guide to _____ (The Entrepreneur's Guide to Customer Development)
- » Discover _____ (Discover Meteor)

You get the idea. It doesn't have to be complicated; it just needs to communicate clearly.

Editing

Mistakes are everywhere. In fact, you'll probably find a couple in this book, despite my best attempts. Thirty thousand words of writing is a lot of opportunity for grammar errors, spelling mistakes, and worst of all, inaccuracies and misstatements.

That's why we need editors. Note the plural. You need multiple editors. When reading your own work you will only catch some of the mistakes. The same goes for another person. Generally, the more eyes on it the better. That doesn't mean you should write a draft and send it off to several people at once. Instead I like to send it to the first editor, make the corrections, then send the revised draft to the next editor.

Look around online for a professional editor or hire a friend. I got lucky that my mother is a professional copyeditor, so it was easy to hire her. For the technical editing find someone in your industry who can catch factual mistakes.

Expert Interview

What's in a Name?

Brandon's first product was an ebook on a topic he knows very well—*Mastering Object-Oriented PHP*. He started without an audience, but used a landing page and detailed blog posts to build a small launch email list. His list may have been small, but it was enough to sell a few thousand dollars' worth in the first day. Read the interview for more details.

An interview with Brandon Savage, author of *Mastering Object-Oriented PHP*

How long did it take you to write your book?

It took me about four months to write my book.

What inspired you to write a book in the first place?

I was inspired by my research that told me people were struggling with object-oriented PHP. The research included blog post readership numbers and questions asked by people on Twitter, Quora, StackOverflow, and other forums.

How much money have you made from your book and over how long?

I've earned approximately $8,900 from my book since it landed December 18, 2012.

How has writing a book changed your business, career, or life?

The book was the first step in launching my business. Once the book was successful it opened the floodgates of products

Expert Interview

I'm building. The book is directly responsible for nearly $4,000 in additional revenue from a class I'm offering (as of this writing). These figures are necessarily small, and my business hasn't fully matured yet, but it's on the right track. As for how it's changed my life, having extra money is a wonderful thing, especially for someone like me who owns an airplane and flies for fun. An expensive hobby needs extra revenue.

What marketing methods were most successful for selling books?

I use direct marketing as well as an email list. I had people sign up to hear about the book, and that list converted right at 25%. My website has also been a huge player in book conversions. I participated in the 30x500 class that Amy Hoy offers, and having the alumni group to review my pitches was wonderful.

How did you distribute your book?

I distributed my book electronically through my website using Digital Product Delivery (getdpd.com) as the distributor.

What was the biggest surprise in the entire process?

The biggest surprise in the entire process was the fact that people would actually pay $39 for my book. I was terrified at the price, but people have been more than happy to buy it. I estimate that lowering the price $20 would only bring in 20% more customers, while reducing my revenue severely. A premium product deserves a premium price, and you can make money off books if you know what you're doing.

Expert Interview

Are there any lessons you would like to share with authors who are just starting out?

I've learned a few lessons along the way that I think are worth sharing.

The first title of my book was *Do This, Not That: Object-Oriented PHP*. The title sucked. I changed it to *Mastering Object-Oriented PHP*. This title worked much better.

Residual sales are where it's really at. Sure, an impressive launch day of $3,000 is cool, but I've made several thousand more from residual sales.

Offering a sale on your book is a great way to drive revenue and capture customers who are on the fence. For example, I ran a weekend sale of my book at 20% off, which generated $1,400 in revenue.

The more your book speaks to the pain of a group of people, the bigger the sales numbers. It's not about audience size; it's about pain point. For example, I bought Nathan Barry's book on building applications because I'm working on a SaaS offering and felt his book addressed my pain. The stronger the pain, the stronger the sales.

I missed out by not offering value-added components with my book. Thirty-nine dollars is a great purchase to win, but a $99 purchase is far better if you can get it. Nathan Barry and Brennan Dunn both do this with their books. My next book, which I'm writing now, will have value-added components that will dramatically improve the revenue I generate.

4

Pricing & Packaging

Proper pricing and packaging is what will make the difference between book revenue that will take you out to dinner and an amount of money that can meaningfully change your financial situation. So pay attention!

The Mistake Nearly All Authors Make

Did you know anyone growing up who wanted to be a writer? If so, you probably remember them being told they couldn't make a living at it. That's where the idea of the poor, starving author comes from. But just because friends and family discourage aspiring authors with expectations of poverty doesn't mean it has to turn out that way.

If you use your writing to teach skills—especially skills that your readers use to make money—then you can make a living through your writing. You just need to follow a few simple rules.

What to Charge?

What should you charge for your book? Let's start by running through a common line of thinking. A standard hardback book costs around $25, but online retailers like Amazon often sell them for $15. Hmmm… so your eBook should be priced at $15. But those books are written by well known authors and are professionally published. Since your book is independently published, you should knock a few dollars off. That brings us down to $12.

Ah, but yours is also just an eBook. Those don't cost anything to distribute each copy, so we should take out those costs as well. Now we are priced at $6 or $7. But then what about those stories of eBooks priced at $2 or $3 that sell millions of copies and the authors become famous and get publishing deals? Maybe $3 is the right price.

This line of reasoning is directly responsible for the poor, starving author.

I have no intention of being a poor, starving author. Do you?

Real Pricing

I think that almost all books are underpriced. The thought process that we talked about earlier drives race-to-the-bot-

Pricing & Packaging

tom thinking that will continue to make books less expensive. That may be fine if you have massive distribution, but I don't. I have a limited audience from a small blog. Even if every one of my readers purchased a $3 book (not going to happen), it wouldn't be financially viable.

So instead of pricing based on what other people are doing (i.e. market pricing), I price based on value delivered. My books are used by software professionals around the world to improve their products. Often these products are used by tens of thousands of customers. By teaching design skills to these professionals, their abilities and ultimately what they produce improves substantially. This means their companies make more money and they get paid more.

Thirty-nine dollars is inexpensive to my target market. So, to justify that price, I need to make sure I can deliver many times that in value.

A Small Audience

Chances are you don't have a huge audience just waiting to purchase your writing. That means you need to make the most of the few fans you can find between now and launching your book.

The mistake authors—and anyone who sells a product online—make is they price low and sell just a few copies, thinking that if they raise the price they will sell fewer copies. True, you will sell fewer copies, but you will still make significantly more revenue.

Price High

Let's use some numbers from my first book, *The App Design Handbook*. In the last nine months the book has sold 724 copies at $39 each. That is $28,236. Not bad, but remember that is over almost year. So what would it have looked like if I had chosen a "normal" eBook price like $9?

Would I have sold four times as many copies? Probably not. I've never tested lowering the price, but for other products I have doubled prices to see how revenue is affected. Typically when I double the price of a product—within a certain range—I lose 25% of the sales. Based on that formula I'm guessing a book at 1/4 the price would sell twice as many copies. So my $9 book could reasonably expect to sell around 1450 copies for a total of $13,050. Ouch. That's a massive loss in revenue.

When you have a small audience you need to charge a higher price in order to make a living.

It's About Value

Now you may object, "Who would pay $39 for an eBook!?"

That's where the value comes in. If your book delivers a huge amount of value, as a book focused on acquiring a valuable skill should, then it is worth paying for. My friend Brennan wrote a book on increasing your freelancing rate. At the $49 price point he charges, the book will pay for itself if the reader can increase their rate—even slightly—with just one client. With Brennan's method that's easy.

Deliver tons of value and charge based on that.

Use Packages

I actually didn't make $28,236 from *The App Design Handbook* as I stated above. I made $49,576.

Where did this massive increase in revenue come from? Well, as mentioned above I priced the book at $39, but what I didn't mention is that I also included more expensive packages with more options.

- » The Book ($39)
- » The Book + Videos ($79)
- » The Complete Package ($169)

The higher packages included video tutorials, Photoshop files, code samples, and additional training materials. Not everyone will upgrade, but enough will to make it totally worthwhile. Here is how the sales broke down for each package:

- » The Book ($39) - Units: 353 Revenue: $12,287
- » The Book + Videos ($79) - Units: 233 Revenue: $16,487
- » The Complete Package ($169) - Units: 138 Revenue: $20,802

The same number of units sold, but with a total revenue of $49,576. That's the power of packages, nearly doubling revenue with the same number of sales. I actually did this with my second book as well, but with higher prices and a stronger top-end package, and it made me even more revenue.

So a higher price—based on value delivered—plus multiple packages can at times increase your revenue by four times. That's how you avoid being a poor, starving author.

Not Everything Should Be Priced High

In March 2012, two design eBooks were released on the same day. *Step-by-Step UI Design* by Sacha Greif was priced at $3 (with a $6 deluxe package) and *Bootstrapping Design* by Jarrod Drysdale was priced at $39. They both had very successful launches and Jason Cohen invited them both to write guest posts on his blog detailing their pricing strategies:

- » Sacha's post
  (http://blog.asmartbear.com/perfect-pricing.html)

- » Jarrod's post
  (http://blog.asmartbear.com/higher-pricing.html)

Just looking at the pricing you may think I like Jarrod's a lot better (since $39 is a price I chose for my book), but I actually like elements of both.

In order to get the complete picture you need to look at the books themselves in more detail. The $3 book is a 42-page case study of designing one specific application, whereas the $39 book is full length and covers a wide range of topics. I believe *Bootstrapping Design* delivers more value than *Step-By-Step UI Design* and should be priced higher. I think Sacha would agree with me.

Price based on value delivered. A small product can have a small price. That's fine. But don't think you are stuck with low pricing.

I should also note that Sacha later increased his pricing to $6 for the eBook and $12 for the deluxe package, which includes source files. I think this is a great price for his product.

Your Goals

Why are you writing this book? Your motivation to become an author doesn't really affect decisions up to this point, but from here on, it becomes really important.

Are you in it to make money? Be perceived as an expert? Get more consulting clients?

All of those are fine, but they heavily affect our distribution methods and pricing.

It's Not Just About the Money

If your goal is to build a huge audience, then a lower price may make a lot of sense. After all, the lower the price, the more copies you will sell. At least that is true most of the time.

Looking back to Sacha and Jarrod, Sacha sold 1,476 copies and Jarrod sold 242 copies in the first 48 hours. Jarrod may have made more money (good), but Sacha has a much larger group of paying customers (also good).

Switching Media

The same information can be taught through several different media. You could use a video, blog post, or podcast episode to all share the same information. The core message doesn't change, just your method of sharing it.

As an author you should try teaching in several different media types.

Some people learn better by listening rather than reading; others prefer reading. Different subjects work better in different media types. It may be complicated to write out a design tutorial and get you to follow it, but I could demonstrate it in 30 seconds with a screen recording.

On a complex subject someone may use both your text and a recording to be clear on how to accomplish a task.

Perceived Value

When selling a product, you can't truly determine what it is worth. After all, value is relative. What you can focus on is perceived value. When selling your book you need to make sure the price matches the buyer's perceived value. Including content in multiple media is a great way to do that.

If I offered one of my design books by itself at one price point, then for a higher price with additional text content, I don't think the perceived value of the second package is very high (remember that these are just perceptions). I think part of the reason for this is that the medium is unchanged.

Instead, if the new content is offered in the form of video tutorials or video lessons, the perceived value increases. Maybe the content could have been provided as text just fine, but to me it feels like it is worth more if both text and video are included.

That's why, for my books, the base package is all text (one medium), the middle package includes some videos and Photoshop files as well (three media), and the top package includes more of the above, plus code samples (four media). This is because each package needs to increase in perceived value to match the price increase.

Examples

Here are a few examples of different media you could try with your product:

- » Short video tips
- » Video Interviews
- » Text interviews
- » Design resources
- » Sample code

» Explanation screencasts

» Video lessons (video of the expert talking)

» Photoshop files

Packaging Matters

PDF eBooks are worth more than blog posts. Something about taking the same content and packaging it as a downloadable PDF makes it feel like it is worth more, even if both are free.

You can then take the same content and record it as a series of video lessons, and watch the perceived value increase.

Patrick Mackenzie took what could have been an eBook (sold for $10 to $40) on email marketing and turned it into a video course that he sold for $497. Same content, different medium. Different perceived value.

Start paying attention to how you personally perceive the value of different product opportunities. Are there specific trends you notice? Can those help you sell a higher-priced product and end up with happier customers?

Free, Paid, or Both?

Getting Real by 37signals and *Rails Tutorial* by Michael Hartl have both made a significant amount of money on their PDF and other versions, but are also available freely online. So

Pricing & Packaging

why would someone pay for content that is available for free? Good question. I was initially skeptical that this would even work and was surprised to hear how successful it has been.

Let's talk about a few benefits for the author in releasing book-quality content for free:

» More people will read your work. Rather than just a few hundred or maybe a thousand people that may buy your book, you can reach a much wider audience. Want to help a lot of people or be seen as a thought leader in your industry? A free version may be the way to go.

» More people will share your work. *Rails Tutorial* has become the de-facto starting point for learning Ruby on Rails. Because it is such a high-quality product, available completely for free, it is linked to and shared all around the web. That means shares on Twitter and Facebook and lots of back-links that help search engines know it is valuable content. Speaking of search engines…

» More content to index. Google can't add the text of your PDF eBook that is behind a paywall to its index. But a free book, available on a web page, can be indexed. That is a lot of content for Google to start serving up to searchers.

So that establishes reasons to give a version away for free, but we are still trying to make money from a book. So how do we get some people to pay for the book?

Here are a few reasons to pay anyway:

» You enjoyed the book and want to support the author. This is surprisingly common. I've been impressed by how many people are eager to support the people who have taught them meaningful things.

» You want the book in a specific format. Both *Rails Tutorial* and *Getting Real* were available for free in webpage form, but if you wanted a PDF or eBook format you needed to purchase a copy. People will pay for convenience. I know many bloggers who sell content in their eBooks that has already been released on their site for free. Just doing the work to package it up nicely is worth quite a bit.

» There is additional content available for paying customers. This is my favorite reason. *Rails Tutorial* offers 20 hours of video tutorials for those who purchase the full version. Many people will enjoy the book and then decide to purchase in order to learn even more.

Remember Pat Flynn with the LEED exam study notes? His eBook was 95% the same content as what was available for free on his site. That just helped his sales.

Interviews

The fastest way to elevate your status and visibility while teaching is to conduct interviews. Interviews are how Andrew

Warner with Mixergy and David Siteman Garland with Rise to the Top have grown large audiences so quickly.

Interviews work so well because they let you leverage the audience of the person you are interviewing and borrow some of their status. Once you publish an interview with Expert A, most likely they will share the interview with their followers, which will drive traffic and attention to you.

Since Expert A trusted you enough to do an interview, you can use that when pitching to Expert B. Once you have a list of quality interviews, people will actually be eager to be on your show. That would be a nice change, wouldn't it?

When I started asking people to do an interview for my book on designing web applications, I was worried about getting rejected. Though that did happen, it wasn't as often as I thought. The most common response was, "Of course, I'd be honored."

That reminded me that even the internet-famous people that I looked up to had been in my position before. For some it was ten years ago, others just two or three years ago. They could relate, and since I had made a genuine pitch, they were happy to help.

Remember that asking to interview someone is a compliment. It means you admire them and their work. If they aren't too busy, most people will accept.

It is important, though, to make sure they don't have to do any work. If you are asking them to fill out an extensive questionnaire, do research before the interview, or prepare something to say, your success rate will be a lot lower. The great thing about interviews is that the interviewee can just show up for a specified amount of time (30 minutes is great) and answer questions. That's a fairly low commitment.

Interviews are also a great way to meet people. It's a casual introduction, you get to talk to them for 30 minutes, and it can be a great lead-in to developing a friendship. You need to do the work to follow up afterwards, but it is well worth it. One of my favorite things about writing and teaching is the people I have met and become friends with along the way.

After the success of my first two books I've had a few people ask to interview me for their podcasts. My response is the same as what I heard from others: "Of course, I would be honored." After all, I'm just excited that people find my work interesting enough to want to hear more about it.

Should You Pay Them?

After seeing the list of people I interviewed for *Designing Web Applications*, quite a few people asked, "How'd you get them to agree to an interview? Did you have to pay them? Was there a revenue-sharing agreement?"

Nope. I never offered and they never asked. Everyone who responded—and several I contacted never responded—was happy to do it for free. I never created any other expectation.

You could offer to pay them something for the 30 minutes or an hour that they will spend with you, but chances are, it will be a lame amount of money. What's that interview worth, one percent of your project? Ten percent?

Jason Fried, the president of 37signals, was one of the people I interviewed. He has a wildly successful software company, a *New York Times* bestselling book, and probably can get paid a huge amount of money for public speaking if he wants to. Do you think the $500 or $1,000 I could offer him (since I didn't know starting out how successful my book would be) would be motivational to him?

Not at all. It wouldn't even be worth his time to set up a simple profit-sharing agreement for that amount of money.

The Open-Source Developer

This type of situation reminds me of talented software developers who spend a lot of their time working for free on open-source software, often working more than 10-20 hours a week after their day job. All for free.

Seeing all this free work, a businessperson will offer the developer $50 to make a small customization to the open-source software for that specific business.

Offers like this are almost always flatly rejected. Why?

Because those developers bill out their time for $150-300 an hour. They are happy to donate their time to the hobby project, but as soon as you bring money into the equation it qualifies as work. Work for an insultingly low amount of money.

How to Approach Interviews

If the expert you are approaching has to do anything more than talk to you for an hour, you should consider working out a joint-venture agreement. But if they don't need to prepare anything, just ask them to do the interview. Make sure they know it is part of a project you plan to sell, but don't bring paying them into the conversation.

I'll bet they won't even ask.

Labels Matter

The labels you use to describe your products are important. You may think that since it's just text content, it doesn't matter what you call it. But it turns out guides or courses are perceived to be more valuable than books. After all, books are everywhere for $12 (or less if they are eBooks).

Traveler and author Chris Guillebeau refers to most of his online products as "guides." His guide on flying for almost free is called "Frequent Flyer Master." At no point does he refer to it as a book, because books aren't worth as much as guides. Instead, this guide commands a price of $49. Since you're guaranteed to get far more value than that from the guide, that is a fair price. He just doesn't want his content to be compared to a book, so he uses a different term.

When I was starting my web design business years ago I purchased a book (effectively) called "The Web Design Business Kit" for about $200. It was shipped to me and came with two large spiral-bound notebooks full of content. The first was all the book-style content (just in a different format); the second was sample proposals, contracts, follow-up messages, and a lot more. Then there was a CD included with digital copies of each of these documents, ready for you to personalize and use for your own business.

The content was great, but it was the high price and "kit" label that made me pay extra attention to it. I don't think I would have paid as much attention to it if it came in the form of a "book." It's strange, but paying more made me get more value from the product.

Courses, guides, kits, lessons, and classes are worth far more than books. Think about how the terms you use to describe your content alter the perceived value.

Consider Preorders

Before I started developing ConvertKit (my latest web application), I talked to a lot of people to see if there was a need for the product. I got a resounding "Yes!" from everyone I talked to.

Now your friends (mine, too) have a habit of saying what you want to hear. So if you ask them if they would use this product the answer is always "Sure. Yeah, I would. It looks cool." If you take that at face value you will think everyone wants to be your customer. The truth is, they are just being your friends. They don't want to tell you they aren't interested or that your idea sucks.

So, you can't trust the opinion of your friends and family. But you can trust their wallets.

Your company will be built on successful payments, not positive opinions. If you want to know what they really think of your product, ask them to pay for it. I don't mean in a generic, "If this product existed, would you buy it?" sort of way… Instead I mean: "I can process credit cards on my iPhone right now. Do you want to preorder my awesome product?"

Let's get back to my ConvertKit story. Like I said, I got lots of positive opinions. I even asked everyone if they would preorder. Most said yes. The problem was I wasn't ready to accept preorders. So I told them I would get back to them.

Turns out, a few weeks later when I was ready to accept preorders, most weren't interested. The two people I was the most sure would preorder never did. They weren't going back on their word. Instead, issues like missing features or it being too much work to switch to another platform became excuses.

That feedback is incredibly valuable, but I didn't get it until I actually asked for money.

Brennan Dunn has used preorders successfully with both his books. For his first book he offered a 20% discount for anyone who preordered. He sold over $10,000 before he launched the book. That provides great validation that your book is in demand. For his second book he leveraged his existing list and customers to gain even more preorders.

Don't trust someone's opinion as validation. Only trust their money.

Piracy and DRM

After the initial splash I made with my first book, *The App Design Handbook*, I received a flurry of questions like this from worried soon-to-be authors: "How do you keep people from sharing and pirating your book?"

That's an easy question to answer. I don't.

There is nothing preventing someone from uploading my books and videos to download sites or distributing them for free. I don't require a purchase number to open the file, have any code that limits the number of computers it can be viewed on, or even add the name of the purchaser to the PDF. In theory, any of these methods would do something to decrease the number of unpaid copies circulating the internet. But it's not worth it.

Digital Rights Management (DRM) such as what I've described above tells all your legitimate customers, the ones that trusted you with their money, you don't trust them. That's not a good message to send.

Instead, I want my customers to know that I trust them with the content. I'm not going to put silly child locks in place that will ultimately just frustrate them. Having to authorize computers or not being able to view something on your phone or tablet are just a few side effects of DRM.

Does It Help?

I don't add DRM because of how it appears to my customers. But let's take it further. Does DRM help prevent piracy? I don't think so. I know from my high school days how easy it is to download software trials from the Adobe website and then add a serial number and some quick code to get yourself the full version for free.

Whatever DRM method you use will be easily bypassed.

Are You Losing Sales?

Probably the most important point of this entire discussion is that those people wouldn't have purchased anyway. You can't take the number of unpaid downloads, multiply it by your sticker price, and claim the result as lost revenue. Those sales never would have happened in the first place.

People who want to pay for your book (the majority) will. Those who don't want to will go without or pirate it. You can't control that. Stop trying.

The worst thing you can do is frustrate the people who have given you money while trying to chase phantom purchases. Instead, spend that time and effort building great products, marketing them effectively, and making your customers happy.

PDF Stamping

A more popular method lately is to have your fulfillment software stamp the name or email address of the purchaser into the PDF. The hope is that people won't be as likely to share something since their name is attached to it.

I used to think this feature was really important. I almost skipped over a great payment provider since they didn't have the feature.

Turns out, it doesn't really matter. Editing the name back out is really easy, so it is a fairly unhelpful form of DRM. Though I will say it isn't inherently bad, unless you make your customers feel like you don't trust them. Then it's lame.

Worse Than Piracy

With *The App Design Handbook* I had an experience that was far worse than someone posting my book for free on a sketchy site. It all started with a confusing email:

"I bought your Kindle version of App Design book from Amazon. There seems to be formatting issues in it. Has anyone mentioned it? Wondering whether there will be a reprint of it."

My first thought was, "Yikes, formatting issues aren't good…" But wait. Amazon? I don't sell my books on Amazon. What's going on? I replied to try to get more information. Surely he meant Gumroad or my site.

But no, he had purchased my book from Amazon and it looked terrible!

> to users to test you will you stay on track and don't break your chain.
>
> quickly discover whether you chose the right So the notifications feature gets included.
>
> features or not. Users will suggest that it should
>
> Now we could say that notification time is **have this or that and you can tell them it is on**
>
> always at 5:00 PM or some other hard-coded the feature list to be added in a future update.
>
> ■value. While it would still work for some it would annoy a lot of other users who have different **By keeping the first version simple you can test** ■more thoroughly, release sooner, and be more uses in mind. So, even though it means adding ■confident in your first version. Your application another screen, we are going to let users set the ■doesn't have to be complex or feature-rich in reminders for any time of day they would like.

This is a screen shot of the poorly formatted Kindle book.

Turns out an enterprising individual named Giorgi Janiashvili also wrote a book titled *The App Design Handbook*, a book that just happens to have the exact same content as my own. Yes, someone was passing off my work as his own and trying to make money from it.

I quickly contacted Amazon (as did the person who alerted me of the issue) and they removed the book from sale. Other than that, there wasn't much to be done. I could try to research the seller, but what would that accomplish?

Ultimately the best thing to do is to focus on the customers who are happy to pay you money and ignore those who try to illegitimately profit from your work. The distraction is just not worth it.

5

Design & Formatting

There are so many formats—and just as many ways to create each one. Which to choose?

Well, they all have pros and cons. Let's walk through them so you can make an educated decision based on your book.

Choosing a Format

The format you choose for your book depends heavily on where you plan to sell it. The iBooks and Nook stores require an ePub file and the Kindle store requires a Mobi file. Now if you are like me and ignore all those platforms, you have more options.

Chances are you will make your book in multiple formats, which is painful no matter how you look at it. Since my books are so design–heavy I chose to release them only as PDF files. These PDFs can be read on just about any device, but they won't be formatted for devices like the iPhone or Android phones. So while they work, they aren't the best experience.

The advantage is that you can fully control the colors, layout, and style of your book. What you create is exactly what the reader will see.

Jarrod Drysdale, the author of *Bootstrapping Design*, also chose to make PDF the primary format for his eBook, but he also included ePub and Mobi formats for Kindle and iBooks. He does include a note saying, "The .ePub and .Mobi formats provide limited control over graphics and typography, and thus are less ideal for a design book."

Clearly he has had people request those formats, but isn't thrilled about how they turned out.

Creating a PDF

PDFs are the best way for your content to be read on traditional computers and tablets, which is why I decided to focus on that format. Once I had made that decision, I thought the rest would be easy. Turns out there are a lot of different ways to create that PDF. Here are the methods I considered:

- » HTML to PDF conversion
- » LaTeX to PDF conversion
- » Microsoft Word
- » Apple Pages (Mac only)
- » Adobe InDesign
- » iBooks Author (Mac only)

That short list is just what I was trying to choose between. I'm sure we could come up with many more options. I started asking around with other authors to find out what they used. Surely one would be far more popular than the others. Turns out, everyone was spread out across the list.

Let's work through them one by one, and then I'll show you what I chose.

HTML to PDF

The idea here is that you make a webpage for each chapter in your book. They can be styled with CSS (Cascading Stylesheets) so it is very easy to consistently apply styles across your entire book. Then when your book is ready you run it through a conversion process to generate a PDF.

This seems to be a great option for books with minimal formatting or technical books that include a lot of code. Another huge advantage is that the ePub and Mobi eBooks formats are HTML based, so including those formats is much easier.

Mathias Meyer used this method for *The Riak Handbook*, a book on using a NoSQL database, and I've heard great comments from plenty of other authors as well. It just won't work well for complicated layouts.

LaTeX to PDF

One option that I haven't tried in detail is to use LaTeX to generate your PDFs. LaTeX is fairly complicated to get started with, but will give you very advanced typesetting and formatting options. You can then use this to generate a PDF file for distribution.

Michael Hartl, author of *Rails Tutorial*, and Garret Dimon, author of *Starting and Sustaining*, used LaTeX to create the PDF versions of their books.

Microsoft Word and Apple Pages

Word and Pages function in basically the same way, so we'll cover them together. These tools are probably the easiest way to get your book written, but they aren't without faults.

You have enough design tools and capabilities to meet most design requirements. Formatting photos and captions can be a bit annoying, but if you don't have too much content, the process is manageable.

Sacha Greif, the author of *Step-by-Step UI Design*, used Pages to design his book.

A huge downside is that both Word and Pages treat your entire book as one giant document, meaning that adding or removing content early on in your book can change the formatting and page break positions all throughout your book. Sacha's book is short, so it is a manageable problem, but in my 150+ page books it would become a nightmare.

If you have a shorter book or minimal design requirements I think Word or Pages are a great way to get your book released.

Adobe InDesign

InDesign is a tool created specifically for laying out print designs. Used by professional designers, InDesign will have everything you need to get exactly the look you want. Since it's designed for the task, you won't have the same annoyances that you would with Word or Pages.

Jarrod Drysdale, the author of *Bootstrapping Design*, used InDesign to lay out his book.

But you should know that Jarrod is a designer and InDesign is a tool made for designers, not for do-it-yourselfers who just want to get their eBook finished. Even though I am quite familiar with the Adobe design suite, I still found myself frustrated by complexities in InDesign.

InDesign is by far the most powerful tool in this list; it just isn't for beginners. If you don't need to do much advanced design in your book, it is probably overkill.

iBooks Author (Mac only)

iBooks Author is the only tool on the list specifically designed for creating eBooks, and it shows. Rather than being one long document (like Word or Pages), iBooks Author splits your book up nicely into chapters and sections. Adding more content extends that section, but doesn't ruin the spacing further on in your book.

You have many different options for page layouts (based on style and number of columns), and setting styles for your entire book is quite easy.

The big caveat is that iBooks Author only comes with a few default styles, so everyone's books look the same, unless you customize your style, which isn't too hard. You have to pick a template to start with, but then you can just start changing the fonts, layout, and colors until you have created something entirely new. Then save that as a template so you can use it for your next book.

There are a couple of websites that will sell iBooks Author templates for quite reasonable prices. One of my favorites is iBooksAuthorTemplates.com. Use the code "authority30" for 30% off your template.

If you haven't picked up on it already, iBooks Author is my favorite tool of the list and what I used for both of my design books. It gives just the right amount of design flexibility in an easy way. I never found myself wishing for a simpler interface or more features. Apple seems to have captured the perfect balance.

Licensing Issues

I initially dismissed iBooks Author because of licensing issues. When Apple released iBooks Author in January 2012 it was targeted at the textbook market and a subset of their iBooks store. Because of this they had language in their license agreement that said whatever content you made with iBooks Author could only be sold in the iBooks store.

Yikes. That's not cool. There was an uproar and no response from Apple. At least that was the last thing I had heard.

Turns out a few months later Apple quietly updated their license agreement to say that .iBooks files, meaning those made in iBooks Author destined for the iBooks store, could only be sold in the iBooks store. But other formats, like PDF, could be distributed elsewhere.

Now that's reasonable. You lose some extra functionality by not using the .iBooks format. Did you see the cool interactive books that Apple demonstrated with that launch? Those features, like embedded movies and 3D models, are only possible in the iBooks format. PDFs can't use that.

So if you choose to sell in the iBooks store you can get extra functionality, but otherwise you can create PDFs to sell anywhere online that have all the functionality of a regular book.

A Web-Based Book

Instead of bundling your book as a downloadable file (like a PDF or ePub), you can build a website specifically for the contents of the book. Note that this is separate from your landing page. This distribution method can work two ways: either you follow the lead of Michael Hartl and 37signals and make a version of your book available for free online, or you can create a membership site or course so that people buy access to your book and view it online.

Either way you will need a web-based, HTML version of your book. Just like for your marketing site, WordPress is the best way to set this up. Each section of your book can be a blog post with categories to organize each chapter. Then create one table of contents page that links to each section (a post) and make it the home page of the site.

You then need to find a WordPress theme that is convenient for reading the content in a book format. The most important features are that you can remove the extra links and fluff that aren't needed and that the theme has clear navigation. It should be very easy to click "next" to move on to the next section in the book. Going back to the table of contents each time you want to move ahead is a bad user experience.

Since your book is hosted on the web you can make an update at any time and everyone will have the latest version. This makes it very easy to fix mistakes and add new content, and it's a great option for the non-technical who just need it to be set up once.

Access

Giving your book away for free can be a great way to gain exposure, but not everyone wants to do it. So to host your book on the web without making it free you need a way to restrict access. There are many WordPress plugins that will run a membership site for you, meaning an account is required to view the content and only those who have paid will have accounts.

This is important because otherwise your content will be available for anyone to read (and search engines to find), regardless of whether they have paid for it or not.

S2Member and Wishlist Member are two popular plugins for setting up these membership sites. Just keep in mind that this method will restrict who you can use to process payments.

Up-Sell

If you do choose to make a version available for free, make sure it has an obvious upsell to additional content. This can either be through an email opt-in form that adds the visitor to an email course—that up-sells after spending time teaching—or a direct link to your sales page to purchase the higher packages.

Just don't give away your hard work for free without having a way to either make money or gain subscribers.

What About Print?

I would like to have physical books to sign, but both my design books have so many screenshots they would cost a lot to print, plus I don't want to have to deal with any fulfillment issues.

The more I look into it though, there seem to be some great options that aren't nearly as expensive as I made them out to be, especially if you have a book that wouldn't require full color (with a bleed) to be printed.

Rob Walling uses Amazon's CreateSpace service to print and ship a paperback of *Start Small, Stay Small*. The book costs about $3 to print and another few dollars to have shipped, meaning each copy only costs $6 to have shipped directly to the customer—all handled on-demand by CreateSpace.

Rob doesn't have to carry any inventory that may not sell or worry about packing and sending orders on time. CreateSpace books are also carried in the Amazon Marketplace, which many people prefer for purchasing.

Spend some time searching for other printers. Just keep in mind that drop shipping (where the printer will ship directly to the customer) will save you a ton of time and will let you go on vacation without worrying that orders won't get shipped out without you there.

Don't underestimate the perceived value of having a print book. They can be sold or given away at conferences, given to your mom, and placed on your coffee table to impress dinner guests.

Besides, it's really hard to sign an eBook for one of your fans.

Designing the Cover

For self-published books, cover design is surprisingly unimportant. Since your book will never sit on the shelf at Barnes & Noble, you don't need a flashy cover in order to draw attention and get it picked up. If you sell in the Amazon or iBooks store, though, you do need to at least think about your cover.

Stick to Basic Elements

If you want to hire a professional designer, that's great. Your book will look even better by doing that, though it isn't necessary. You can create a great cover yourself by just sticking to a few basic elements.

» **Color:** I like to choose one bold color to serve as the background for the book cover. Blue for *Designing Web Applications*, orange (my favorite color) for *The App Design Handbook*, and green for this book. If you don't know what you are doing, don't mix multiple colors.

» **Type:** Choosing a bad font is where most cover designers go wrong. Go for something strong and classic. When in doubt, Helvetica, Georgia, or Arial are all just fine. Stick to one or two fonts at most. Don't try to get fancy.

» **Good spacing & alignment:** Make sure that all the elements on your cover have space. Crowding your design is the easiest way to make it look amateurish. You also need to make the alignment consistent. Having slight differences in the space between your elements and the edge of the book will look really bad.

The publishing company Five Simple Steps uses very simple covers for all of their books. A solid color and good typography are enough to add credibility to their books. Trust me, they aren't hurting for sales.

Adding Imagery

If you want to get a bit fancier, the easiest thing to do is add an icon. Solid color, outline-style icons work really well. The *Designing Web Applications* cover looked too plain with just the text and background color, so I added a browser icon.

That is a custom icon, but they don't have to be. The Noun Project has a very large collection of flat icons

that work well. I used their typewriter icon for the Authority book cover.

A Pattern

Finally, on each of my book covers I add a simple background pattern. Acquired from SubtlePatterns.com, these patterns just add a bit more detail. For *Authority* I used a collection of random typographic characters. You can choose from hundreds of patterns; just make sure you keep the end result subtle. It's really easy to overdo the design.

Page Orientation

For *The App Design Handbook* I made a dumb mistake in my design. Can you spot it on the sales page?

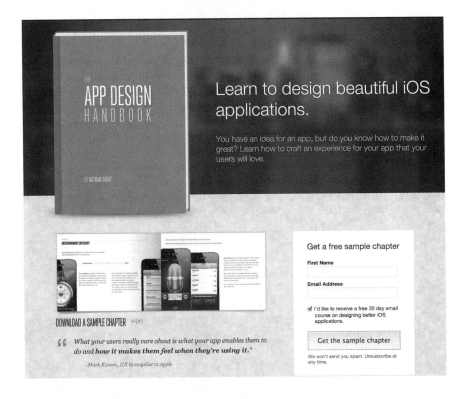

I actually didn't notice until my friend and fellow designer/author, Sacha Greif, pointed it out. My book, as shown in the sample chapter screenshot, is in a landscape format. So if there were a physical copy it would be wider than it is tall, like a coffee table book. But my book cover screenshot clearly shows a portrait book. Oops!

No one besides Sacha has said anything, so I haven't fixed it yet. But it's a silly issue that got me thinking about whether a book should be portrait or landscape.

Portrait or Landscape?

Every tool I mentioned earlier can work in either orientation, so there aren't any real restrictions for using one over the other. If your book has a lot of screenshots, as my design books do, then you will have an easier time laying them out in a landscape orientation. If it is mostly text, portrait works better for reading straight through.

It comes down to personal preference, but in general a landscape book will require more layout effort to make it look good. You can create a more interesting layout with multiple columns, pull quotes, and photos worked in, but it may not be worth the effort for your book.

Whichever you choose, make the book cover mockup match the format of your actual book. Not that your readers will notice, but it's nice to get the little details right.

> Expert Interview

A Lucrative Hobby

Mike Rundle had built a small following of iOS designers and developers from the free tutorials on his blog, but he never expected to make the amount of money he did—enough to help him get his dream home faster. How's that for publishing some tutorials?

Mike was kind enough to sit down for an interview and get into more details.

How long did it take you to write your tutorials?

The first Design Then Code tutorial (http://designthencode.com/scratch), which is free and is sort of like a prerequisite for the other ones, took awhile, a few months at a solid few hours per day, mostly at night after work and on weekends. I decided that I really needed to write a free introduction to building iPhone apps if I wanted to sell tutorials that were at an intermediate or advanced level, else I'd never get beginners to latch on and understand any of the more interesting things I was trying to teach.

It was a lot more time consuming to write and edit because the concepts I was rolling through weren't just step-by-step instructions on building an interface or constructing an iPhone app, but the fundamental concepts of developing software for the iPhone, Objective-C, and its unique and potentially scary syntax, and getting readers in the right mindset to develop iPhone apps the way Apple likes you to develop them.

> **Expert Interview**

My wife, a software engineer who doesn't write iPhone apps, was really instrumental in the editing process because she constantly read the tutorial and would tell me which parts weren't clear and how to make it friendlier to people who were advanced in another language. I was also poring over various other "introduction to Objective-C" tutorials/books that others have written to see where I thought they were less than clear, and where I could provide some additional color or information.

The current tutorial (Texture) took less time than the introductory one, probably about two months at one to two hours per day, again mostly at night and on the weekend. Writing the tutorials is fairly straightforward. The initial ideation time to figure out what I want to design for it is the fun and more time consuming part. My next two tutorials (which, in my opinion, are a lot better than the current Texture one!) I've been working on in parallel for about two to three months, at maybe three to four hours per week if I'm lucky. Both the design and apps are built at this point; the next step is writing the tutorials for each one, which should go fairly quickly since I am essentially just describing the steps I already went through to produce the design and working app.

What inspired you to write them in the first place?

Well, it's a blessing and a curse to be able to do all design and all development work for an iPhone, Mac, or iPad app by myself, which is the odd skill that I have. I've been a designer and a programmer at the same time since I was a young teenager, so I've always had the ability to work on "the whole project"

Expert Interview

from start to finish, across a number of platforms. The reason I said that sometimes it's a curse is because, as someone who can dream up an app and then design and build and finish it, there's really no limit to what you can do, there's no waiting on someone else to build it or anything. Unfortunately, that also means that you can randomly start a million things and never finish them!

So, to be honest, I'm terrible at finishing apps. Since the iPhone came out, I've probably started and stopped 15-20 different apps, each left at various levels of unfinishedness — sometimes 5% or 10%, other ones at 50% or 60% — and I stop working on them because my passion waned or I just couldn't see the light at the end of the tunnel anymore. Lots of different genres too: puzzle games, kids' animated games, Twitter apps, news and information apps, mood/entertainment apps, etc.

So after spending a few years starting and not finishing a number of apps, I had a bit of an epiphany, and that was instead of trying to start and finish an app and launch and market it, why not teach others how to design and build apps? Why not "sell your by-product" as Jason Fried has said (http://37signals.com/svn/posts/1620-sell-your-by-products) and instead of trying to finish and sell an app on my own, just teach others how to design and build simple apps?

That's what I'm doing, and the best part for me is that I have no problems designing and building a simple 1-2 screen app, as my passion and excitement carry me through. And then in

Expert Interview

tutorial form that's really all I want to teach, end-to-end design and development of simple 1-2 screen apps. Realistically I could take my 15-20 unfinished apps and turn them all into full Design Then Code tutorials, which is something I'd really love to do.

Also, there's really a great niche for tutorials that teach someone how to start with a blank canvas in Photoshop and design an app (one or two screens) and then start with a blank project in Xcode and totally build that app. When I started Design Then Code a few years ago, there was nothing out there that showed a project end to end, and from what I've seen, there still really isn't. There are a bunch of sites that sell UI templates that developers can use in their apps so they don't have to design anything, but not much that actually shows you how to design *and* build an app, from scratch. So that niche is still there and I'm working hard to crank out more tutorials.

How much money have you made from the tutorials and over how long?

The first Design Then Code tutorial launched in March 2011 and I made over $8,000 the first month, which pretty much blew my mind. A few months later I released my second tutorial, which was an all-design focused one discussing lighting and realism in UI design, and it made over $2,000 the first day it was available.

Between July 2011 and February 2013 I'm embarrassed to say that I really didn't do anything with Design Then Code other than update the tutorials a bit to account for newer versions

Expert Interview

of Xcode, but all told I've made about $53,000 from Design Then Code. I didn't do much with Design Then Code (much = anything) in 2012 just because life got in the way and I was busy doing this or that, but the awesome thing about selling something like an e-book online is that it just keeps on selling, so I was still making money.

A few months ago I decided to take it more seriously and work harder on Design Then Code, so I'm excited to say I have two awesome Design Then code tutorials coming in the next month or so, and a totally redesigned site to boot. It'd be great to re-create the sales trajectory from the initial launch again, so we'll just have to see what happens.

How has writing these tutorials changed your business or career?

In a very direct way, Design Then Code helped my wife and me get into our dream home faster.

It made me a lot of money without a lot of upkeep or effort spent (after the initial effort) and still has a gigantic amount of potential. That's why I've been working hard on new tutorials the past few months, because I finally realized what a gem Design Then Code is for my financial situation and career, and I think that I'm just at the beginning of its potential. Lots more people are trying to learn iPhone development each day, and lots of developers are still trying to figure out how to make their apps look great without hiring a designer, and my tutorials work for both those audiences.

Expert Interview

Design Then Code has also helped put me into a position in the iOS design and development community of someone who "knows what they are talking about," which is amazing and humbling since I've only been developing in Objective-C since around 2009. I've been asked to be the author of a number of iPhone development books (always turn them down, though, because why wouldn't I just self-publish?!) and have spoken at conferences around the world with material derived from Design Then Code tutorials.

My free Design Then Code tutorial "Building iOS Apps From Scratch" has been read by over 400,000 unique people since it went live in 2011, so knowing that I've helped almost half a million people learn iOS development is pretty special on its own.

What marketing methods were most successful for selling the tutorials?

My most successful marketing method has been email marketing, and before the first tutorial launched I had a splash page up to accept email addresses. I think when the first tutorial went live I had about 2,000 people signed up, so of course I notified them and had a really high open rate. I've been collecting email addresses since launch and now I have about 11,000 people on the announcement list who I'll be notifying when the next tutorials are available.

I can't really call it "marketing," but just having a Twitter account with lots of followers who are solidly in my target market has been instrumental as well. I don't actively try to

Expert Interview

gain followers, but it's really helpful to have people that you know and trust who can help promote something when the time is right. When the initial tutorials launched, I had some really amazing, high-profile designers helping to promote it whom I met and became friends with through Twitter. So even though I don't pay to promote tweets on Twitter or actively position myself as some kind of social media marketing person, it's great to help spread the word when I finally had something special and important to share with other designers and developers.

I also helped out my friends at Stack Overflow with some design work in exchange for advertising space based on some targeted keywords. I didn't track the impressions and click-throughs on the ads (doh!) but CPC advertising and tracking the funnel down to purchase is really something I've been looking into and evaluating. If you can spend $5 CPC and can consistently convert one out of 10 clicks into a purchase for a $70 book, you're essentially printing money. The key is getting really great at converting!

What was the biggest surprise in the entire process?

I think the biggest surprise is that initially I thought that designers would come to the site and buy development tutorials, and developers would come and purchase design tutorials, but that's totally not the case. Even though you can buy just the design tutorial or development tutorial separately, the vast majority of people buy both, regardless of if they can already design or code well. That really surprised me, and is spurring me in the next version of the site coming over the

Expert Interview

summer to just sell one version of the tutorial, the design and code bundle, and that's it, no way to split it up. I think it makes the most sense that way, and it's also easier to explain how to transition between a Photoshop mockup and the code with regards to slicing up assets out of the PSD and importing them into Xcode.

Another surprise is just how well Design Then Code has been received by people trying to learn iPhone development. A number of top apps in the App Store have been written by people who started out a few years ago reading my tutorials, and that's really humbling, especially when they come to me for advice before they ship because they learned iPhone development from my work.

Is there anything you would do differently?

If I look back now at the launch, I think I did pretty well for not really knowing what I was getting into, but I wish I kept at it and wrote lots more tutorials instead of trying my hand at various apps, and not finishing them. In my case it's been more satisfying and rewarding to work on tutorials instead of full apps because not only do I still make money from it, but I'm helping others learn what I think is valuable, and that's how to craft elegant designs and apps. But I'm rectifying that issue now and am really committed to finishing more and better tutorials soon, and am excited about re-launching Design Then Code in the summer months.

6

Prepping for Launch

How you handle the launch will make every difference for book sales. Even authors with large followings hear crickets when they don't follow a proper launch sequence.

Distribution

Most authors have a "write it and sales will come" approach to their books. The wannabe author assumes that once they write the book the publisher will take care of the marketing, promotion, and sales. That's simply not true. All the successful authors I know have taken full responsibility for the promotion of their books. And that's when they have publishers.

The self-published equivalent is to submit the book to the Kindle or iBooks stores and wait for the sales to roll in. That's a bad idea, at least if you want to make any money from your book.

That's actually one reason I avoid using those eBook stores for my books: not using them forces me to do all the marketing and promotion myself, without falling into the trap of relying on the few sales I may get "for free" just by being in the store.

Selling on Your Own Site

When using another site for distribution, it is too easy to think that all you have to do is write your book and then wait to go viral and hit the bestseller lists on those sites. That's like waiting for someone else to pick you. It's not worth waiting for.

Instead, know that you have to do the marketing as well. When you sell on your own site it is clear that there won't be a magic success that will sell thousands of copies. You have to do it yourself.

That's not to say you shouldn't sell on other sites; just don't start with them or rely on them.

Teasing Draft Content

Remember that landing page we built? Well, hopefully people signed up to hear about your book. That's good. The bad thing is what usually happens afterwards: nothing. That is, at least until the book comes out. Then there is a sudden announcement email and the subscribers are left trying to remember how this random author (that's you) got their email address.

Not good at all.

Pitches from random people don't convert well.

Instead you need to stay in contact with your subscribers. Not every day, but often enough that they remember who you are and stay excited about your book. Once every week or two is great. I know it's hard when you are trying to get the book together, but it's worth it.

Gradually drip out a sample chapter, the book outline, quotes of what other people are saying about the book, and anything else you can share about the process. Try to be helpful and interesting. Most of all, just keep them engaged.

When it comes time for the book launch you want them to remember who you are and already be primed to buy. Oh, and give them a time-limited discount (I use 24 hours) for being a fan since the beginning. Rewards are always good.

A Big Splash

In December 2010 Tim Ferriss, author of *The 4-Hour Work Week*, came out with a new book titled *The 4-Hour Body*. If you read blogs at that time in Tim's target market, you were practically guaranteed to read something about his book. It seems logical to partner with fitness blogs to get them to review the book. That's what any author would try, but Tim took it a step further by tailoring content to each audience.

For the software company 37signals, which publishes a popular software and business blog, Tim wrote an article on how he used Basecamp and Highrise, two 37signals products, to write *The 4-Hour Body*. This article is highly relevant to the 37signals audience, who all use or are thinking of using those products, but it also serves as a subtle plug for his book.

For each site Tim approached, he didn't pitch generic content or just an excerpt from his book. After all, a tech news site may not be interested in that. But he found an angle so that his content was relevant.

Tim also worked with popular fitness sites like BodyBuilding.com to publish fitness-related content.

The goal with this approach is to be everywhere on your launch day. Someone may see a friend link to your book on Twitter, but not pay attention. But if later they are reading their favorite blog and see an article written by you, they may actually take notice. Finally, they may come across an excerpt from your book on an entirely different site and actually purchase it.

Putting It Into Practice

After watching Tim use this for his launch (and even more so for his latest book, *The 4-Hour Chef*), I decided to try it on a smaller scale for my launch of *Designing Web Applications*.

My book is targeted at designers and developers, so writing guest posts for those types of sites is obvious. But that audience doesn't exclusively read those blogs. They also read productivity, business, and lifestyle blogs. So I worked on content for the entire range.

Here is the combined list of non-design or tech-related blog posts I wrote for both my book launches:

1. Are You Making the Most Common Pricing Mistake? (ThinkTraffic)
2. Make Money from a Low-Traffic Blog (ProBlogger)
3. How to Use a Daily Reminder iPhone App to Write a Book (LifeHack)
4. From App Store Newbie to $35,000+ in Profit (ThinkTraffic)
5. Why I Quit My Job to Design iPhone Apps (PocketChanged)
6. 10 Tips For Successfully Marketing iOS Apps (SpeckyBoy)

I didn't achieve the same range or volume of posts as Tim Ferriss, but the strategy did work. I made a big splash in a small corner of the internet. I even received emails from a handful of people who had come across every one of my posts.

It helps a lot to have all the posts go live on the same day (launch day), but that doesn't always work out.

Getting Guest Posts

Now that we've covered the high-level strategy, actually landing the guest posts comes down to quality content and relationships. The more people you know, the easier this is. Start by making a list of sites you would like to guest post on (it helps if you already read those sites), then make a list of the writer or editor for each one.

If you have time, start building up a relationship slowly. Start by leaving helpful comments on their blog posts and starting small conversations on Twitter. Then, after they have seen your name come up a few times, send a helpful email. A great option is to link to another post you think they will find interesting.

Here's a sample:

> John,
>
> I really enjoyed your last post on _____. As I researched the topic more I came across this post that provides some more detail and approaches the problem from a different angle. Here you go: _____.
>
> Thanks again,
>
> Nathan

You didn't ask for anything. You just tried to be genuinely helpful by providing relevant information. That's the key: it must be relevant, otherwise to them you are just sending a random link.

A Foundation

You haven't actually built a relationship yet, but you have laid the groundwork for one to start. Eventually you can approach them with your offer for a guest post. I like to include the post title and a short description of the post. It must be very useful and targeted to that audience, and must not come across as a sales message.

Give them an easy way out at the end. It's not a good idea to hard sell someone you don't know well. If this post isn't interesting to them you want to be able to continue to build a relationship rather than betting everything on this one post.

Affiliates

An affiliate relationship is where you find another person with an audience who would be interested in your book and pay them a portion of every sale. This keeps them motivated to promote your book and you both make money.

On digital books a typical affiliate commission is around 50%. That may seem high, but remember: as the author, you don't have any ongoing costs. The affiliate brings you the sale (most of the work) and you gain a new fan. Overall, it's a pretty good deal.

In order to help keep their affiliates motivated, many authors will even offer a higher commission. The more you do to help make your affiliate successful, the more they will want to promote your book. That's where negotiating the lowest possible commission may not actually be in your best interest.

Most Sales Will Come from a Few Affiliates

Not all affiliates are created equal. In fact, the majority won't make you any money. Most likely 90% of your affiliate sales will come from less than 10% of your affiliates. To make it worse, you have a hard time controlling exactly how your books are promoted, meaning some of these affiliates may use methods you don't approve of or do yourself.

The point is, be very selective of who can sell your product.

Chris Guillebeau fixes these issues by making all potential affiliates fill out an application detailing how they plan to promote his books. This lets him mitigate what he calls the 98/2 rule—where only 2% of your affiliates ever sell a single copy.

Chris now has a much smaller group of affiliates to focus on answering their questions and helping them sell more copies.

Make your affiliates an exclusive group; fire anyone who uses questionable sales techniques.

Are You Only Recommending This Because It Makes You Money?

Once you start an affiliate relationship people will question their motives for promoting your book. What may have seemed before like a genuine testimonial now may seem like they are promoting it to make money, which is partially true.

Only work with affiliates you think genuinely like your product, but know that even then they will get some flack from their audience. Especially if it is handled poorly.

Preview Copies

A great way to get attention for your book is to give away preview copies to friends and influencers. Garrett Dimon recently did this with his book *Starting and Sustaining*, which is about bootstrapping a software-as-a-service business. At the time I didn't know him well, but I knew of his work and we had talked a couple times.

When he sent me a preview copy of his book asking for feedback, I was thrilled to help. After reading a few chapters, I could provide (hopefully) meaningful feedback to improve the book. He incorporated those changes and got me an updated copy.

So the first point is that you can use that feedback from preview copies to release a better product.

Helping with Launch

Just as importantly, when *Starting and Sustaining* was released, I was far more likely to promote it since I now knew Garrett and felt like I had a tiny part in helping with his book. This meant I tweeted about it a few times and shared it with friends. I don't know if I generated any sales for him, but at the very least I caused a few more people to view his work.

Testimonials

For my first book, *The App Design Handbook*, I didn't give away any preview copies. I should have, but I was working on the book up until launch day (don't do that) and I didn't feel comfortable sending out a draft. That's something I should have gotten over. Just tell your reviewers that you are still working on finishing up the formatting and final details, so they should focus their feedback on the content and overall message.

Because I didn't overcome my fear of sharing a draft product, I didn't have any testimonials when it came time to launch. A few interested visitors emailed me saying the book looked great, but they were on the fence about purchasing. Did I have reviews from happy customers?

Oops. I didn't.

Garrett didn't have that problem. He was able to launch with quite the list of positive comments from influential bloggers who had read at least part of his drafts.

These testimonials contributed to the social proof and his sales site, and I am sure they helped increase sales.

Don't Expect Too Much

Always keep in mind that people are busy, especially bloggers who have big audiences. Here are two tips to help get a response:

Do It in Two Steps

Don't just email them a copy of the book. First send a very short email explaining who you are and the project you are working on. Ask if they would be interested in a review copy.

Make sure they understand you don't expect anything from them. If they are busy they can look it over or ignore it.

Then if they respond positively, send over the draft. Your results will improve significantly. The less you ask of them the easier it is to get a buy-in. Once you have that soft commitment from them they will be much more likely to actually help you.

Target the Content

When Tim Ferriss (whom no one had heard of at the time) tried to get bloggers to review his first book, *The 4-Hour Work Week*, he didn't send them the entire thing. Instead he found one chapter that he thought his target would find particularly interesting and sent them only that.

One chapter or section is a lot less intimidating to read than the entire book. Since he targeted his content and his pitch to each person individually, his results improved significantly.

Asking for Testimonials

Now about those testimonials. If you want them, you need to ask. It's really rare that busy people will volunteer good testimonials about your work. In the publishing world it is very common for authors to write endorsements for each other's books. For example, best-selling author Seth Godin has given testimonials for dozens of other books by upcoming authors.

In fact, when one friend noticed how many books had an endorsement from Seth Godin on the cover, he said his book would be unique by not having Seth say something nice about it.

The point is, don't be afraid to ask.

Write for Them

My friend Brennan Dunn used the pricing strategy I outlined earlier in this book quite successfully. Instead of waiting for him to offer a testimonial without prompting, I wrote one for him:

"Nathan's pricing strategies made me an extra $15,000 from my self-published book."

I knew that statement to be true (from private conversations) so I wrote it out, sent it to him, asking him to sign off on it. Brennan took the time to write a longer testimonial, but what I sent him set the tone for what I wanted him to say.

That's an easy way to get great testimonials. You get a higher-quality endorsement and your reviewers only have to approve what you've written instead of writing it themselves.

Giveaways

Constantly promoting a single product to your audience can become tiring, for you, but especially for everyone who listens to you. Doing giveaways is an easy way to continue talking about the same product, without saying anything new, while still delivering value.

Since your product is digital, giveaways don't cost you anything, except you may lose a customer that might have purchased your product. If they like the product, they'll tell their friends, so I don't see it as much of a loss.

The easiest way to do a giveaway is have everyone post a comment to enter, then use a random number generator to pick a comment at random. Then email the winner.

Sometimes other related sites are willing to do giveaways to their audience. It's a good way to get some more exposure without having to write a full guest post.

When App Advice did a review of my iPhone app Commit they gave away a single copy to commenters. The comments exploded: nearly 100 comments from readers trying to win a 99-cent app. I guess people really love free stuff!

7

The Sales Page

You wrote a book people care about and found an audience interested in reading it, so now let's convince them to part with their hard-earned cash.

Focus on the Pain

A good sales page spends the first few seconds getting the visitor interested, then the rest of the time overcoming objections that keep the visitor from making a purchase. A complicated or expensive product can have a lot of objections, so keep in mind that you may have to write a lot of content to make the visitor feel comfortable with the purchase.

The more I am asking from a user, the longer I make the sales page. That means I ask for email addresses on a short landing page and sell $249 products on long, detailed sales pages.

The Pain

A good product solves a painful problem. You need to talk to your customers to find exactly what those pains are so that you can write to them. When writing the sales page for this book, I asked my Twitter followers (you could ask your email list), "What is your biggest obstacle keeping you from writing a book?"

The answers came pouring in: "discipline," "time," "self-confidence," "an audience," "insecurity," "fear of not making sales," and "not enough time."

These are all objections that I hope I've helped you overcome throughout this book, but having them listed out like that practically wrote the sales page for me. I took each of these problems keeping my readers from reaching their goals and wrote them in a list. Then I wrote a narrative for each, explaining my methods—the methods spelled out in the book—for overcoming each one.

The goal is to convince each visitor to the sales page that I am speaking to them directly since they likely have some of these same issues to overcome as well. As they read through your sales page they should be thinking, "Wow, he really understands me." That's how it feels when you speak to the same pains that your visitors are feeling.

Writing The Sales Page

Note that I said earlier that I wrote the sales page. I didn't say designed. Design is important, but that comes later. First you need to open up a text document and write out the entire page. The common mistake is to start with design, then write sales copy to fill in the blanks. That's not going to work well to sell products.

Instead, use a text editor to force yourself to ignore the design entirely. Write a narrative that overcomes every objection your buyer might have while gradually leading them towards buying your product.

Only after you have the text written should you start adding design and visual elements. If you can't design the page yourself, don't despair. A pre-written sales page is much easier for another designer to turn into something that looks good (meaning you save money). After all, you've already done the hard part.

Basic Elements

These basic elements are required for just about every sales page, so make sure to include them:

- » Why someone should care about your book
- » A sample chapter
- » The table of contents
- » Social proof

- » About the author
- » Listing your packages
- » A purchase option
- » FAQ to overcome more objections
- » Another purchase link

A Sample Chapter

Based on conversations with potential buyers, having a sample chapter as a quick, free download is really helpful for customers deciding whether or not to buy. They can immediately get a look at the actual content, formatted the way they will be reading it. Even though it is just a portion of the book, it goes a long way towards building trust in the final product.

This sample doesn't need to be a single chapter. You can pull a few of your favorite sections from different parts of the book together. Just enough to give a feel for design style, readability, and what experience level you are teaching to.

Just make sure it is really high quality. Your book will be judged on this sample chapter more than anything else.

Frequently Asked Questions
(magically written in advance)

A good landing page spends the entire copy overcoming objections. Is this for me? Is the source credible? Will it solve my problem? What if it doesn't help me?

The Sales Page

Inevitably there will be some objections that you can't answer in the main sales copy. That's why I love an FAQ, except that no one has asked you those questions before, so I guess they aren't frequently asked.

Use this section as a bucket to answer anything about file types, a refund policy, and skill-level expectations for the reader. But remember, this is still sales copy. Use it to convince potential buyers who need that extra push.

After you actually receive some questions, add those, along with the answers, to the FAQ. Every question is an objection to the sale. Make it easy for your visitors to contact you. Otherwise, they will be thinking those objections without a way to tell you.

Tips

Include an image that physically represents the product. This is why so many eBooks (mine included) show the book design as a printed book, even though a printed version doesn't exist. This helps instantly give the visitor an idea of what the page is about.

You don't know where your visitors are coming from, so don't assume they already know about you or your book. Start from scratch and make it immediately clear what your sales page is about.

Social Proof

Social proof is a method of building trust by implying that other people like your product. Testimonials are a very obvious form of social proof, but even the Facebook "Like" button is adding social proof when it says, "seven of your friends like this page." If seven people like it, then it must be good.

More popular authors can use the same concept when they quote the number of books sold as a way to hint at the quality of the book.

Testimonials are the easiest form of social proof. I hope you've been gathering them from each person who previewed your book. There are two mistakes most commonly made with testimonials:

1. The testimonials are plain text and don't include a photo.

2. The testimonials are all lumped together in a single section of the page.

Have you ever read a sales page with glowing testimonials and wondered if those people really exist? "John Smith" could have been made up on the spot to try to add credibility to the product.

By adding a photo, job title, and link to the name, you help prove to the reader that your endorsements come from real people, not just from your imaginary friends.

It is also important to mix the testimonials throughout the page where they have the best context. When talking about how your product solves a specific, painful problem, it is even more powerful to follow it up with a testimonial saying that your product really did solve the pain.

Other forms of social proof include logos of companies you've done work for, news organizations you've been featured in, and prominent companies using your product.

8

E-Commerce

Choosing a platform to sell your book is a great place to waste a ton of time. Just read this section and make a decision, then move on. If you already have a preferred method, feel free to skip this section.

Overview

Once your sales page is in place you need a way to actually accept payment. You can build it directly into your site (a bit complicated) or link to a third party provider (much easier). If you are new to the process I recommend using a provider that can be integrated with just a link. The most common are PayPal, Gumroad (my favorite), SpaceBox, and E-junkie. More on each one later.

Kindle

When asked what I do, my standard response is something like, "I'm a software designer, but I've also written a couple of books." They always respond, "Like printed books?" "Nope. Just self-published eBooks."

"Ah," they respond, as they start to lose interest. "Do you sell on Amazon?"

As crazy as it sounds, I don't sell on Amazon, just on my own website. Now this acquaintance doesn't know how to relate to what I do. I don't fit into any of his preconceived boxes and am now quite a long way from what he would consider a respectable author. It's too much work to explain that I make a respectable living from my books in part because I keep them off Amazon.

The Kindle Store

The Amazon Kindle promises your eBook will be available to purchase on millions of devices, so it's the default choice for nearly all self-published authors. It has a lot of great things going for it:

1. **Great distribution.** You can read on all the Kindle devices as well as in the Kindle app for iOS.

2. **Open to self-publishers.** Getting set up is very easy. You don't even need an ISBN.

3. **A marketplace for readers to find your work.** Amazon is a search engine just like Google and Bing, except that people searching on Amazon are expecting to make a purchase rather than get content for free. That's a good thing.

There are downsides as well, notably pricing and owning your customer list, but depending on your goals, Amazon may be a great fit.

The Setup

Getting started is really easy. Just visit kdp.amazon.com and sign in with your existing Amazon account. Agree to a contract and you can immediately create your book. The process for everything else is pretty straightforward. Just fill in the title, description, categories, and a bit more information before uploading your book file. I didn't run into any issues other than creating the actual file.

Creating Your .Mobi File

Amazon uses the .mobi eBook format, which is based on standard HTML. Since your book will be viewed on everything from the black and white E Ink classic Kindle to the brilliant iPad display, there isn't much formatting you can do, primarily just headings, images, bold, and italics.

You will need to download the Kindle Previewer application to test what your book looks like on different devices. It isn't perfect—so you should definitely test on an actual device—but you can be confident most of the formatting is in place.

It may be worthwhile to hire a freelancer for a few hundred dollars to do the formatting for you. Elance.com would be a great place to start.

Also note that you may want to create a .mobi file even if you don't plan to sell through Amazon. You can bundle the eBook with the rest of the files sold through your own site and let the buyer copy it over to their own Kindle.

A Note on KDP Select

Amazon's KDP Select program will grant you extra distribution, slightly improved royalties, and pay you every time the book is borrowed. The only catch is that your book must be exclusive to Amazon for at least 90 days.

If your goal is to reach a big audience, this may be useful, but exclusive distribution to Amazon goes against so much else in this book. You wouldn't be able to sell on your own site, price the way you want, or own your customer list.

Plenty of authors recommend using Amazon to distribute their book, but I don't know anyone who makes the majority of their money on Amazon for a book they are actively promoting. That's why I stay away from selling on Amazon.

iBooks

The iBooks store gives you access to a huge number of devices and potential customers, but like any other platform, it isn't reasonable to expect they will do the marketing for you. If you get a sales bump from being in the store, that's great. But don't count on it.

Pricing Restrictions

Apple takes a 30% cut of your sales regardless of price. The only restriction for selling books in the iBooks store is that your price must be $15 or below. Depending on your goals, this could be a deal breaker. It was for me with my first two books.

Two Types of Files

One thing that confuses new authors about the iBooks store is the difference between standard eBooks versus eBooks created with iBooks Author. I love iBooks Author for creating my PDF books, but it is mainly designed for creating textbooks, a subset of the .iBooks format that is specific to the iPad. This means that the iBooks file you create with iBooks Author can only be viewed on the iPad and not on the iPhone or iPod Touch.

For access to all devices you need to use a more traditional eBook format like an ePub. That doesn't have the same formatting options that iBooks Author gives you, but the content will flow nicely regardless of the screen size.

A Seller's Account

To start the publishing process on the iBooks store you need to apply with your Apple ID. The Apple ID you use has two strict requirements:

1. It must have a valid credit card tied to it.

2. It must not already be tied to an existing iTunes Connect account (such as for selling iOS apps).

The first requirement is easy, but the second requirement meant I needed to create a new Apple ID just for this, since I already sell iOS apps.

Apply

Next, you need to apply for access to sell on the iBooks store. This is just a form asking for your name, Apple ID, and password. Very easy. I'm not sure why they have you apply, since you don't give them enough information for them to make a real decision on whether or not your content is good.

Anyway, once you fill out the application form, you wait. I wish I could give you a timeframe, but it seems to vary a lot. Several people have reported times as short as 24 hours, others around three days. Unfortunately, after nearly a week I still hadn't heard anything back on my application.

So I emailed ibookstore@apple.com to find out what was going on. They just said my application was still processing… Not very descriptive, but ten minutes later I got an email welcoming me to the iBooks store. I doubt that was pure chance.

So if your application takes more than a day or two, send Apple an email.

Contracts & Banking

After your account is approved you need to sign in to iTunes Connect (http://itunesconnect.apple.com) and start agreeing to contracts. Once the contracts are taken care of, add all your contact information and finally your bank account information so that Apple can pay you for the royalties.

Publish

To actually publish to the iBooks store you need to use a free tool called iTunes Composer. This rather clunky desktop app will walk you through setting the pricing, adding a description, and getting all the other details in place to publish to the store.

Just go through each step and fill in the necessary information. The tool is quite good at telling you what it is missing or where the errors are.

...Or You Don't Have To

Keep in mind that selling through the Kindle or iBooks stores is completely optional. I've made a significant amount of money even though my books are nowhere to be found on either store. For my goals, controlling pricing and owning the customer list are worth more than any sales I would make from being in these marketplaces.

Gumroad

My favorite delivery platform is Gumroad. I've used Gumroad to sell all of my digital products and haven't ever looked back. Gumroad has, without a doubt, the best checkout experience on the web. Since I sell books about designing a great user experience, it would be hypocritical of me to use a provider that didn't have a good checkout experience.

Sahil Lavingia, the founder of Gumroad, describes his mission for Gumroad to make selling a digital product as easy as sharing a link. And he's done a fantastic job.

Setup

Setting up Gumroad involves filling out just two fields: email address and password. With that information your account is created and you can start adding products. If you want you can instead sign in with your Twitter or Facebook account.

Once your account is created you can immediately add your first product. For this only three things are needed: the product name, a file (you can enter a URL or upload a file), and a price. Fill those out, click the checkmark, and your product will be created.

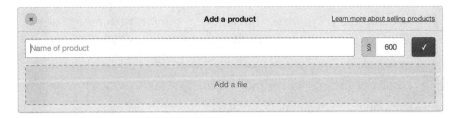

Details

Once the basic product is created you can add some more details like a cover photo and a description. Once it looks good click Publish and you are ready to start selling.

You can also configure options to allow discount codes (which Gumroad calls "Offers"), add custom fields to the purchase form, limit the number of copies available for sale, and even add variations customers can choose from.

Pay What You Want

One of my favorite features is "pay what you want" pricing. When filling out the price box you can add any number. For example, "10" means you are selling your product for $10. But if you write "10+" then customers can pay $10 or any higher amount they want. So you can distribute your book for free with "0+" and some customers will happily pay you more for it.

It's a nice, simple feature with a clever user interface.

Integration

When it comes time to integrate Gumroad into your site you have two options: a link to their site or the embedded modal.

The link is quite straightforward. Simply copy and paste the URL to your product on Gumroad. The disadvantage is that customers will be taken away from your site when they go to purchase.

If you use the modal (which is just as easy to integrate), then the Gumroad product will be loaded in an overlay window above the rest of the page content. The rest of the checkout process works the same, except the customer never leaves your site.

For those who are technically minded, the Gumroad purchase happens entirely in an SSL secured iFrame, meaning you don't have to worry about setting up SSL encryption on your own site. You really just drop in their code and it is secure by default.

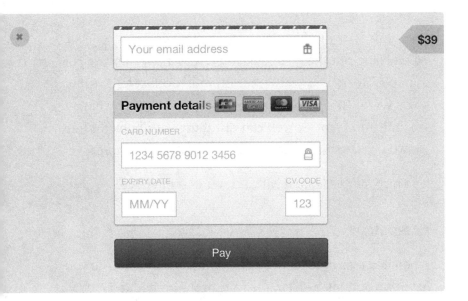

Purchase

The purchase experience is where Gumroad really shines. When making a purchase online most e-commerce platforms ask for every possible bit of information: first name, last name, email address, physical address, company name, credit card number, name on the card, billing address, security code, expiration date, and anything else they think they might need.

Gumroad lets you purchase by answering just four fields: email address, credit card number, expiration date, and security code.

They don't even ask for your name or address.

It's great. Customers can get through the purchase form with minimal hassle and you will look great, since your product uses the best checkout experience on the web.

Customer Support

No matter which platform you choose you will run into issues. Guaranteed. That's why good customer support is so important.

I've always received prompt replies and helpful information from the Gumroad team. They were even helping me upload files at midnight the day before my first book launched.

Gumroad really is a great product put out by a wonderful team.

Downsides

Every product has faults. With Gumroad they are not so much faults as just features I wish they had. For example, I'd really like to be able to integrate a third-party system like KISSmetrics or Visual Website Optimizer to optimize my conversion rates. Unfortunately, Gumroad doesn't have a way to do this, meaning I can't effectively A/B test changes to my sales pages—at least without writing custom code to use their webhooks. Obviously, this hasn't prevented me from selling my books, but it would be really nice to have.

Affiliate support is also missing, though I hear this is coming at some point.

At one point I also wished for the ability to add coupon codes for products, but they just launched that feature. So the team is working hard to build out all the functionality you may want, but they prioritize user experience over a lengthy feature list, which, if you've read either of my design books, is a very good thing.

Details:

- » Merchant Account: included
- » Fee: 5% + $0.25
- » Setup: Instant
- » Affiliate support: none
- » Payment details: direct deposit every two weeks

PayPal

For most sellers online PayPal is still the default way to collect money. Just about everyone has used PayPal before in one way or another. And their opinion seems to be split between "They are okay" and "I hate them."

Frozen Accounts

When Gumroad first started they didn't have direct deposit payments into your bank account—they do now—so they would transfer you your money through PayPal. This worked fine for months and I moved over $60,000 from Gumroad—through PayPal—to my bank account.

Gumroad let me know that they had just released their own direct deposit, so my latest payment (of $20,000) would be the last one to go through PayPal. The day after that money was safely in my bank account, PayPal froze my account. It took over a month of back and forth negotiations to get the account unfrozen. Luckily I only had a few hundred dollars in PayPal since my large transfer had just cleared.

Do a little searching around the internet and you will find no shortage of sellers who hate PayPal and will never do business with them again. There are just as many that had their accounts frozen, worked through the issues, and still use PayPal—but are careful to keep their current balance small.

Call Them

If you do get your account frozen don't waste time going through PayPal's online forms. Just find the contact page and call them. Issues that took a month of back and forth emails were resolved in 30 minutes on the phone. It's a pain, but way better than waiting months to get your money.

Someone Will Ask to Pay with PayPal

Despite all the bad things I said about PayPal, I still let people buy my books this way. Why? Because someone always asks. Either they don't have a credit card (or they are purchasing from a country that blocks credit card payments to your country) or they prefer PayPal over using their credit card online. There will always be someone who needs an alternate payment method.

My friend and fellow author, Sacha Greif, lets his customers choose whether to use a credit card (processed through Gumroad) or PayPal when they check out. Most choose the credit card, but this is a seamless way to let the customers choose whichever method is easiest and gives them the most confidence.

A Warning

By their nature, eBooks sell a lot on their launch day. You may not hit $10,000 or $20,000, but if done well you will go from no sales to a lot of sales in a very short time. This is the kind of thing that sets off alarm bells with a payment processor. That's why I work with Gumroad, a team small enough to be aware of my specific situation and who will talk to me before taking any drastic actions like freezing an account.

E-junkie

E-junkie has been around a long time and has helped many successful authors get their start. Unfortunately, it's been around a very long time and is starting to show its age. If you want a specific feature, E-junkie probably has it, but wrapped in an interface that was considered cutting edge ten years ago. On the web that's a long time.

E-junkie also only handles the shopping cart, file delivery, and administration part of the transaction. You will still need to use either PayPal or Google Checkout to collect money.

Affiliates

The biggest reason E-junkie is still around and doing well is their affiliate system. If you want to have affiliates sell your product, E-junkie is the leading platform. They have many thousands of affiliates ready to sell just about any product, making it very easy to get started.

Unfortunately, they are willing to sell just about any product, so don't expect a very high-quality affiliate relationship.

Space Box

Space Box, like Gumroad, is a new player in the payment and file delivery space. The downside is that they lack features (like affiliates) that many have come to expect. On the upside, their user experience is awesome. Maybe not quite as good as Gumroad's, but probably only user experience designers would really notice the difference.

Space Box + Stripe

One nice thing about Gumroad is that you sign up for a single service and it takes care of everything for you. No need to get a separate merchant account, which is usually required for processing credit cards.

Space Box doesn't handle payment, but they integrate very nicely with Stripe, which includes your merchant account. So the two services combined are still much simpler than a traditional merchant account setup for processing cards.

The Fees

If you are very conscious of paying credit card fees, but still want a nice interface, then Space Box is a great option. Since they process fees separately you just have to pay 3.9% + $0.30 per transaction. So this is a bit cheaper than Gumroad at 5% + $0.25 per transaction.

Had I used Space Box instead of Gumroad for my last $142,000 in book sales, I would have saved about $1,485 in fees.

WordPress Plugins

There are many WordPress plugins that will let you integrate sales directly onto your site. Some work really well, though for selling a book I don't recommend using any of them.

Having the checkout process on your own site adds a lot of complexity and opportunity for mistakes without giving that much value. These can be a turnoff for your potential customers. On the other hand, very few customers will cancel their purchase because you send them to an outside payment provider like PayPal.

The Cart Problem

My least favorite thing about e-commerce platforms is that they use a shopping cart, meaning they assume the customer is going to purchase multiple items, so they add products to a cart before checking out. This makes sense for large sites, but is just confusing if you only sell a single product (a book and its variations).

By cutting out the cart you can avoid confusion from the additional steps.

Security

By sending customers to an offsite purchase process you offload all of the security risk so that you don't have to purchase and install an SSL (Secure Sockets Layer) certificate and maintain your own security. This is a big deal when you are handling credit cards. Mistakes can be expensive.

If you know what you are doing, great. Otherwise use an offsite provider and let the experts worry about it.

The Gumroad Modal

Gumroad is an offsite provider (which has security benefits), but they also let you embed the purchase process in your site through the Gumroad modal (a better user experience). This is essentially the best of both worlds: the security of an offsite process with the trust and seamless checkout process of an onsite e-commerce platform.

It's the exact method I use to sell my books.

9

The Launch and Beyond

All this work comes down to one moment of hitting the publish button on your sales page. But then an entirely new world opens up.

Launching Your Book

Everything that we just spent so much time covering comes down to a single moment—or rather a moment that kicks off an entirely new journey. Chances are you won't just hit publish and then sit back and rake in money, though if you've done things right sales will come.

The Day Before

If you have done your work to this point, you've been in touch with your email list on a regular basis. It's crucial that you aren't a stranger to them. Just to be sure, send an email the day before that makes the launch date and time very clear.

Your entire list should be crystal clear as to when your book is available.

In fact, you want them to make their purchase decision by the day before at the latest. That way when the announcement email comes on launch day all they need to do is get out their credit card. The subscriber who has been hearing about your book for the last few weeks should not receive the launch email and try to decide then whether or not to buy. If that happens, they will probably put off the decision until later and then not purchase at all.

Don't worry about the unsubscribes you will get from this email; those people weren't going to purchase anyway.

Final Tests

Look over all the details for your launch. Your landing page should be up on a test site with all the e-commerce links and functionality in place. Go through and test in all major browsers. The last thing you want is a simple bug preventing purchases.

Look through the files you are having delivered. Is everything there? Any last minute mistakes to fix?

Once everything looks good, write your launch email. Don't try to be clever with the subject line. You need it to be very clear that the book your list has been waiting for is now ready, and that they should go purchase it right now.

When there is nothing left to tweak or fix, go to bed. Tomorrow will be a big day, so you want to be awake and ready for it.

Launch Day

I always get up early so I can launch at 8:00 a.m. Eastern time. Since I live in Mountain time, that means I need to launch at 6:00 a.m.

The first thing to do is move your sales page to its final URL. I like to replace the email opt-in page with the sales page. That way any old links will now point directly to the sales page. Test everything again to make sure the move didn't break any functionality.

Now check your analytics and make sure that the tracking code is working on your sales page. It would be annoying to have incomplete statistics.

Publish a post on your blog. The content should be a summary of what the book is about, along with a strong call to action to purchase. This should be a good article for someone who may not have been following along with every step of the process, as your email subscribers have. It doesn't need to be too long since your sales page will cover everything they need to know.

Hit Send

The next step is to re-read your launch email. Hopefully you can find a few easy ways to improve from last night. Once it looks good, hit send—and wait.

Both of my previous books had sales within the first ten minutes. Depending on the size of the list and how well primed customers are to buy, yours may take longer. Now get up and get some coffee or make breakfast before you sit down and start the real work for the day.

Asking for Shares

Hitting publish was the easier part. Now it's time to hustle and ask all your friends and connections for help. Write out a draft email that can be customized for each person you need to contact. Here's a sample:

Authority Is Live, Can You Help?

> Hey _____,
>
> Thanks so much for your help and support through this process. It means a lot! The book is finally live and sales have started to roll in. You can check out the site here:
>
> [Link]
>
> Would you mind helping me promote the book? Tweets, Facebook posts, and Hacker News submissions are all welcome. I appreciate all the help. :)
>
> Let me know if I can help on your next project.
>
> -Nathan

The Launch and Beyond

Make It As Easy As Possible

My friend Barrett Brooks recently launched a new book called *Career Kickstarter*. In his announcement email to friends asking them to share the book he included sample tweets, making it as easy as possible to share:

- » My friend, @BarrettaBrooks, just launched Career Kickstarter, The Complete Guide to Finding a Job that Matters. http://www.careerkickstarter.com

- » Looking for a job? Find a job that matters with @LivingforMonday's Career Kickstarter. http://www.careerkickstarter.com

- » If you could do anything in the world for work, what would you do? @LivingforMonday's Career Kickstarter will help: http://www.careerkickstarter.com

- » Do the hard work to find your dream job. This guide offers a step by step process: http://www.careerkickstarter.com (Via @LivingforMonday)

- » Check this out from @Barrettabrooks & @Livingformonday. 2 years in the making... All to help you find your dream job. http://www.careerkickstarter.com

All I had to do was scan the list, find my favorite, tweak a few words, then paste it into Twitter. Deciding what to say is a tiny roadblock, but you want to do anything possible to make your request easier.

Who to Contact?

I like to start by sending an email like what we just talked about to everyone I interviewed for the book. Since they are considered experts, chances are they have large followings which would be interested in their interviews. The reach you can have just from asking interviewees to share makes it worth doing the interviews just by itself—ignoring the value they add to your product.

Once you've contacted everyone you interviewed, reach out to anyone else you know with a related audience. If you contacted these people for testimonials, that's good. The more interactions you've had, the better.

Finally, ask any friends who would be happy to help. Even shares from people with small audiences can help drive sales.

Just don't be afraid to ask.

Check on Guest Posts

With the bulk of your emailing out of the way, check up on any guest posts scheduled to go live today. If the post hasn't gone live yet, consider sending the editor or site owner a quick message to see if something went wrong. Chances are it is just scheduled for later in the day, but it doesn't hurt to ask.

A lot of my guest posts were on sites hosted in Europe or elsewhere around the world, so my launch day and time varied.

Just keep time zones in mind with everything regarding your launch.

Walk Away

Refreshing your sales stats, responding to comments, and checking real-time analytics isn't a good way to spend your entire day. Go do something else. Keep checking back every hour or so, but don't spend all day in front of the computer. Beyond a certain point there isn't much more you can do to increase sales, so take a break.

You deserve it.

Authority

The Dip

If you plan for a big launch (like you should), then sales will probably never be as high as that first week. Just by their nature book sales start high and decrease over time. The trick is to get your base sales to stay at an acceptable number. That number will depend on your goals and audience size.

My goal is to maintain $5,000/month in revenue from each of my books. But your launch efforts will only carry you so far. You need to continue building and teaching your audience in order to keep making sales.

A month ago I had my worst week of sales ever. Instead of making a few hundred dollars a day off of each book, I went days without making a single sale. The week total was $216. The drop off was sudden enough that I checked the sales page to make sure something hadn't gone down, but everything seemed to be working fine. Traffic was down a little bit, but not enough to match the sales drop.

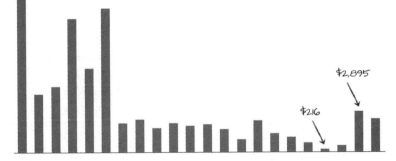

After talking with a few friends about it they informed me that this is normal. Sometimes you will have a bad week. Get over it. The bigger issue is the decline over time. So don't get caught up in sales for a single day or week, but look at the trend over months.

Still, a dip like that was a serious concern. Looking at the weekly sales graph you can see a significant decline.

A Fix

"When was the last time you wrote about design?"

That's the question that got me thinking. I'd been writing a new blog post at least every week, but lately they had been on marketing, effective email, and productivity. Everything but design.

Realizing the issue, I wrote a new design-focused article that had a soft-sell for *Designing Web Applications* at the end of it. The result? An instant jump in sales of $1,200 that day.

When sales drop, keep teaching and giving content away for free in order to reach new people and remind your existing audience about your products.

Creating Courses

This is where we take our basic email strategy from the book launch and turn it into an advanced system that will continue to sell books—in an automated way—for years to come. If you haven't already launched your book, don't worry about this part. It's not really worth setting up until after launch.

Automated Teaching

I hope that by now you've learned that teaching is an incredibly effective marketing method. I've used it to generate hundreds of thousands of dollars in sales, and others have used it with even more success.

Here's the problem: I often feel like the effort put into a single blog post only provides temporary value. The blog post gets traffic for your readers at the time, but gradually becomes buried. You can feature a few of your best posts in your sidebar, but that's still not great.

The problem is even worse with emails. If you write a great email and send it to your list, only those subscribers at that moment will get it. All new subscribers miss it entirely.

That's where email sequences (or courses, as I call them) come in. Take a collection of your favorite content and set it up to go to new subscribers at certain intervals. When a user first subscribes they will receive a series of your best content spread out over several days. This gives a great introduction to your new readers and makes sure that your favorite articles don't get buried.

Building Trust...

Imagine you and I meet at a cocktail party for the first time. After quick introductions I discover you are interested in writing books. If I were to immediately follow that with, "Oh! I wrote a book about self-publishing. You should buy it!" How do you think that would go over?

Yeah, not well. Trying to sell you on products before you have any reason to trust me does not go over well. In my fictional example you would try to find the least awkward, but still quick, way to exit that conversation.

The same thing happens all the time on the web. You click a link in a Tweet and end up on a sales page. You don't know the product, the seller, or have any reason to trust them. You exit the conversation by hitting the back button. It really is just like our in-person example. That's why conversion rates are typically so low.

...So That You Can Sell

What if we incorporated our sales message for the book into our email course? The sales pitch becomes automatic, but only after you've taught the reader a significant amount. Then you move from being a creepy person at a random party to being a trusted advisor.

For *Designing Web Applications* I have an email course that goes out to all new subscribers. The series goes out gradually over 30 days. All emails are educational (and very useful). Note which emails include a sales pitch:

1. Trimming down features

2. Learning to wireframe

3. Designing blank slate screens (soft sell)

4. Think about designing forms in a new way

5. Designing form fields and labels

6. Take your web app design to the next level (hard sell)

7. Adding style to your application design

8. Typography basics (soft sell)

So I wait until the third email to even mention my product. And even then it is in a "P.S." at the end. Then the next email goes back to purely educational. Later an email is a dedicated hard sell, but is followed by a soft-sell.

This process takes time to make the sale—up to 30 days in some cases—but since it is automated, I don't worry so long as it increases conversion rates (it does). If you decide to set this up, use ConvertKit (my email marketing company), as it is designed for this exact process.

Releasing Updates

Your book will have mistakes, meaning you will have to update it. Not only that, but if you write about anything technical, the book will quickly become out of date.

It's not worth worrying about too much before you launch, but just have a basic idea for how updates will be handled. If you sell through a marketplace you can just upload the new version and let the customers upgrade when they want. Selling through your own site you already have their email address, so it is trivial to inform everyone of the new version and where to download it.

Managing Mistakes

Since I use email so much my customers always know how to contact me, meaning they are kind enough to point out typos and other mistakes. There will be some. I don't care how perfect your writing is; you won't be able to release a flawless book.

I like to take the emails that mention mistakes and mark them with a Gmail label called "Typos." This way I don't go make a fix and upload a new version every time an issue is found, but when they start to build up I know exactly where to look for everything that needs to be fixed.

Should You Charge for Updates?

Whether or not you charge for updates depends on the type of book and the expectations of your customers. My preference is to make minor updates and fixes free, but new versions should be paid—with a substantial discount (up to 50%) for people who have already purchased.

It can be really easy to make promises like "updates will always be free!" to your customers, but keep in mind what you are promising. If you write a technical book on a topic that changes every year you just committed yourself to a massive, unpaid writing project each year.

Michael Hartl, the author of *The Ruby on Rails Tutorial*, has to update his book every year for the new version of Ruby. But he charges for updates so he sees a nice spike in revenue for the extra work he puts in.

Don't underestimate the amount of work an update will be. The last thing you want to do is create an expectation that you can't fulfill.

If always-paid updates doesn't sound like something your customers would like, consider giving free updates for a year. I just find that after releasing a book the last thing I want to do is go rework and rerelease sections of it.

Deals & Partners

At some point you will reach the end of your own audience and need to turn to other circles to continue making sales. Conveniently there are communities already out there eager to promote your product… for a portion of the sales.

With the popularity of daily deal sites like Groupon and Living Social (for traditional merchants) many similar sites for digital goods have sprung up. Usually they target a specific niche audience such as design, fitness, or marketing.

I've done promotions with AppSumo (the largest), Dealotto, and MightyDeals. I recommend all three, with some caveats.

Make Them Your Customer

If you go down this path you need to have a long-term approach. The wrong thing to do is throw up a deal, enjoy the quick cash, and move on. Instead you should focus on adding these new customers to your community. To do that you need to be able to contact them.

By default with each of these sites you just get sales numbers and a check. This means that the customer belongs to the seller, not to you. If you recall, that's why I chose not to publish with the Kindle or iBooks stores. To be successful long term, the purchaser needs to become your customer as well.

So I always negotiate the terms of the deal so that I get the customer's email address. In my experience the deal site has a privacy policy that prevents them from handing over the customer list, so you need to set up something a bit more advanced.

I use MailChimp or ConvertKit to set up a landing page that thanks them for purchasing and asks them to enter their email address in order to receive the download. Then it has an opt-in checkbox for them to receive future articles or tutorials from me for free.

Once they enter their email address they immediately receive the book in their inbox. It's a pretty simple system, but it makes it easy to collect email addresses from your customers.

Don't Upset Your Biggest Fans

The people most excited for your book eagerly purchased it on launch day. How upset would they be if the next week it was up on a deal site for 50% off?

I find that waiting several months after launch to run a deal is the best way to avoid upsetting your loyal fans. People expect that products will go on sale; it's just frustrating to have that happen right after you make your purchase.

Negotiate the Royalties

Talk to one of these companies and I bet you'll be surprised at what the royalties are. A 70/30 split is quite common. And no, that's not 70% to you. Your share is the 30%.

Before you get upset and start ranting about how you wrote the book and deserve the larger cut, let's take a step back and look at your margins. Since your product is all digital you should be running close to 95% profit margins on every sale. That means each additional copy sold carries very little additional cost. So you could run this deal at those margins and still make it worthwhile (especially if you are gaining a long-term customer).

But you don't have to. If you've made a good product that the deal site wants to carry it is easy to negotiate down to a 60/40 split or even 50/50. I've done 50/50 splits with both AppSumo and MightyDeals. It just took a few rounds of negotiation.

Diluting Your Brand

Remember how we talked about how price affects perceived value? The higher the price, the more people assume it is worth. Usually that works in your favor. But heavily discounting your product can make it not seem as valuable. Just know that is a tradeoff you have to consider.

That's why I usually won't run a sale at more than 50% off. I feel that any lower than that shows I don't believe my product is worth it.

Know how your products are perceived and make sure that a sale like this won't damage your brand.

Up-sell and Cross-sell

These deals aren't going to make you rich. They'll provide a nice little bundle of cash and hopefully some new readers. But there are a few things you can do to make more money in the long term.

First, I like to run a deal for the lowest package I offer. Usually that is just the book for $19 (normally $39), making my cut $9.50. This way I get more people to purchase, since it is a lower-priced product. The end result is more people hear about me and join my mailing list.

Next, I let customers know that if they want one of the higher packages to contact me for an upgrade. I extend the same discount (50% off) to those who want to upgrade. The difference is that this is a much higher-margin product ($125, normally $249), and I keep all the proceeds.

Finally, once they are a part of my community I can eventually promote other books, workshops, or software applications. The point is I expect to make far more than that original $9.50 off of each customer.

That's why it is so important to make sure they become your customer (not just the deal site's customer).

My Deals

I've run a series of deals with each of the companies mentioned above. Here are the terms and sales numbers from each.

The App Design Handbook on AppSumo

- » Middle package (50% off)
- » 60/40 revenue split (40% to me)
- » ~$5700 in sales
- » 373 copies sold
- » 8 refunds

The App Design Handbook on **Dealotto**

- » Complete package (at least 50% off)
- » Deal price: between free and $84
- » 20 copies sold
- » Profit: $822.40

Designing Web Applications on **AppSumo**

- » Just the book for $19 (50% off)
- » 50/50 revenue split
- » 899 copies sold
- » ~$8540 in profit to me
- » 8 refunds

Designing Web Applications on **Mighty Deals**

- » Just the book for $19 (50% off)
- » 50/50 revenue split
- » 343 copies sold
- » $3138 in profit paid to me

All told I have made nearly $20,000 from running these deals—not including what I made from up-sells to higher packages. Not bad. But more importantly I picked up over 1,500 new email subscribers, which I value just as much.

Up-Selling & Cross-Selling

Throughout this book there has been a huge focus on using email to sell products. Email works really well for the initial marketing and launch, but it's even better as a long-term strategy.

Once sales start to dry up you need to start turning to other revenue sources if you want your business to continue to make money. Having a customer list means you don't have to start from scratch with each new product.

Up-Sells

The first thing to try is an up-sell. If you have multiple packages, which you really should, you can offer the higher package to those who purchased the basic package at a discount. Since you have their email addresses this is an easy pitch to make.

In my experience, though, it won't convert very well since those who purchased the base package chose that originally. There's a good chance they probably can't afford or aren't interested in your higher-priced offerings. It's still worth doing, as I have made at least $500 for each book I tried it with.

Future Products

Once you write another book or build a new product, you can offer that to all your customers. Over 100 people who purchased *The App Design Handbook* also purchased *Designing*

Web Applications. So even though they target a slightly different audience, there was quite a bit of overlap.

In the future I could offer a video course on Photoshop or some other related product.

It doesn't just have to be a book. Brennan Dunn sells a book called *Double Your Freelancing Rate*, but he also runs a software-as-a-service application for freelancers called Planscope. By cross-selling between the two he can significantly increase his revenue per customer.

Workshops

A few friends have doubled their book revenue by hosting online workshops targeted at a smaller subset of their audience. Brandon Savage made about $10,000 in four months of sales from *Mastering Object-Oriented PHP*, but then made an additional $9,000 off his first workshop. He plans to host plenty more.

Brennan Dunn, whose email strategies we covered earlier, has made nearly $90,000 from two books targeted at freelancers in the last year, but has made an additional $95,000 from hosting workshops to help freelancers build profitable agencies.

As you can see, your first book is just the beginning.

Could You Teach a Workshop?

Think of more niche topics that you could teach to your book audience. Is there a topic you could go into a lot more detail on for those who want to become experts in it? If so, an online webinar or workshop could be a great way to teach—and significantly increase your revenue.

At prices between $200 and $1200 per ticket you don't need to sell very many seats before it becomes worthwhile.

Refunds

Even if you write a great book, a few people will ask for refunds. Don't question the quality of your product unless refunds are more than four or five per 100 copies sold (5%). The trick is to not worry about it. Just issue the refund quickly and move on. It may be helpful to briefly ask why they want a refund. Some feedback may help you improve the product in the future.

10

Closing Thoughts

There are just a few ideas I want to leave you with before you jump into writing, promoting, and selling your own book.

The Lifestyle

My one-and-a-half-year-old son, Oliver, has been to more countries than most of my friends. A five-week trip through Europe, plus shorter trips to Canada and Costa Rica, have made for a decent list for one so young.

Two weeks ago, we were on vacation in Costa Rica, and now I am writing this from the lanai at my condo on the island of Kauai. As far as I know "lanai" is just the Hawaiian word for deck or porch. It just sounds better. Anyway, back to the current setting. There is a waterfall 30 feet away and a cool breeze. It turns out working from the beach, the idyllic scenario you hear about, isn't very effective (sun, sand, etc.), but working from the deck of your condo is great.

The point is not to brag. That's not productive.

A few years ago when I worked at a startup I would submit time-off requests for each trip I wanted to take. I hate time-off requests. Something about the process of having to ask permission to spend a long weekend with my family really frustrates me. The company would (almost) always approve the request (they were great that way), but it was slightly grudgingly. They made sure I was aware that my team would need me while I was gone and that other deadlines were really important.

The most important thing writing books has given me is freedom. I haven't submitted a time-off request in over a year and a half. When I want to go on a trip, I just go, without having to ask permission.

Another friend—who loves his full-time job—used a portion of his book profits to buy a Porsche. He'd been dreaming of owning that car since he was a kid; writing a book is what finally gave him the extra money to make his dream happen.

Your biggest benefit from writing a book may be a pay increase, offers for speaking gigs, getting out of debt, or the freedom to travel. I don't know. But I can tell you there will be benefits.

Creative Freedom

An interview with Brett Kelly, author of *Evernote Essentials*, left me with a thought that I want to pass on. He said that when self-publishing, it is your project. You don't have editors or a publisher telling you what can and cannot go into the project.

Closing Thoughts

This means that you can write the book you want, not what anyone else makes you do.

Take that creative freedom and use it to make the best possible book. Enjoy it. Traditional publishers don't give you the same luxury.

Start Before You Feel Ready

My friend James Clear talks about a trait that is found in nearly all successful entrepreneurs, and I'm sure published authors have it, too. This one idea will take you further than most of the specific advice in this book:

Start before you feel ready.

You may not feel like an expert qualified to write your book. But if you don't start, you won't ever become that expert. You may not feel like your audience is large enough for you to actually make a living from your book, but without starting, your audience won't grow.

And finally you may not feel like your work is good enough to charge for it. That's fine. Charge anyway.

To be successful you need to get in the habit of starting before you feel ready.

That one habit will change everything.

Notes:

Authority

Notes

Authority

Notes

Authority